Android Application Programming with OpenCV

Build Android apps to capture, manipulate, and track objects in 2D and 3D

Joseph Howse

PUBLISHING

BIRMINGHAM - MUMBAI

Android Application Programming with OpenCV

First published: September 2013

Production Reference: 1180913

Published by Packt Publishing Ltd.
Livery Place
35 Livery Street
Birmingham B3 2PB, UK.

ISBN 978-1-84969-520-6

www.packtpub.com

Cover Image by Ankita Jha (ankitajha17@gmail.com)

Credits

Author

Joseph Howse

Reviewers

Karan Kedar Balkar

Rohit Bhat

Viral Parekh

Acquisition Editors

Nikhil Karkal

Kartikey Pandey

Commissioning Editor

Harsha Bharwani

Technical Editors

Jinesh Kampani

Manal Pednekar

Project Coordinator

Amigya Khurana

Proofreader

Amy Guest

Indexer

Rekha Nair

Graphics

Ronak Dhruv

Production Coordinator

Conidon Miranda

Cover Work

Conidon Miranda

About the Author

Joseph Howse might be at home right now, sitting on a sofa and writing a book, or he might have dashed away with a suitcase full of books, cameras, and computers. He is equipped to "see the world" or at least to do his work in computer vision.

He is a software developer at Ad-Dispatch (Canada), where he makes augmented reality games for iOS and Android. Thanks to computer vision, the games can make use of real-world props such as a child's drawings, toys, or blanket-forts.

He also provides training and consulting services. He is currently consulting at Market Beat (El Salvador) on an embedded systems project that uses OpenCV for face recognition.

He holds three masters degrees in Computer Science, International Development Studies, and Business Administration (Dalhousie University, Canada). His research has been published by **ISMAR (International Symposium on Mixed and Augmented Realities)**, and he would love to meet you there if you go.

Android Application Programming with OpenCV is Joe's second book with Packt. His first book, *OpenCV Computer Vision with Python*, includes an introduction to face tracking and depth cameras (for example, Kinect) on Windows, Mac, and Linux.

Joe likes cats, kittens, oceans, and seas. Felines and saline water sustain him. He lives with his multi-species family in Halifax, on Canada's Atlantic coast.

I am able to write – and to enjoy writing – because I am constantly encouraged by the memory of Sam and by the companionship of Mom, Dad, and the cats. They are my fundamentals.

I am indebted to my editors and reviewers for guiding this book to completion. Their professionalism, courtesy, good judgment, and passion for books are much appreciated.

About the Reviewers

Karan Kedar Balkar has been working as an independent Android application developer since the past four years. Born and brought up in Mumbai, he holds a bachelor degree in Computer Engineering. He has written over 50 programming tutorials on his personal blog (http://karanbalkar.com), covering popular technologies and frameworks.

At present, he is working as a software engineer. He has been trained on various technologies including Java, Oracle, and .NET. Apart from being passionate about technology, he loves to write poems and travel to different places. He likes listening to music and enjoys playing the guitar.

Firstly, I would like to thank my parents for their constant support and encouragement. I would also like to thank my friends Srivatsan Iyer, Ajit Pillai, and Prasaanth Neelakandan for always inspiring and motivating me.

I would like to express my deepest gratitude to Packt Publishing for giving me a chance to be a part of the reviewing process.

Rohit Bhat is a Computer Science graduate from BITS Pilani, India, currently working as a Software Specialist in a leading Big Data Analytics firm. He has done projects in a variety of fields of technology encompassing Data Mining, Android Development, Open CV, Swarm Intelligence, Workflow Automation, and Video Conferencing platform. He loves to keep himself abreast of the latest technology and can always be found ready for a discussion on any topic under the sun. He is also interested in reading, startup, economics, and current affairs. He likes to write and is a freelance blogger in his spare time.

He is currently writing a book for Packt on Bonita Open Solution, a technology which he has used extensively for Workflow Automation and Business Process Modeling.

Viral Parekh is a young graduate of Computer Science. He is a skilled mobile application developer. He has a grip on the various open source libraries such as OpenCV, OpenNI (Open Natural Interaction), FFmpeg, and video4linux. He is keen to work in the field of Human computer Interaction and Augmented reality.

www.PacktPub.com

Support files, eBooks, discount offers and more

You might want to visit www.PacktPub.com for support files and downloads related to your book.

Did you know that Packt offers eBook versions of every book published, with PDF and ePub files available? You can upgrade to the eBook version at www.PacktPub.com and as a print book customer, you are entitled to a discount on the eBook copy. Get in touch with us at service@packtpub.com for more details.

At www.PacktPub.com, you can also read a collection of free technical articles, sign up for a range of free newsletters and receive exclusive discounts and offers on Packt books and eBooks.

http://PacktLib.PacktPub.com

Do you need instant solutions to your IT questions? PacktLib is Packt's online digital book library. Here, you can access, read and search across Packt's entire library of books.

Why Subscribe?

- Fully searchable across every book published by Packt
- Copy and paste, print and bookmark content
- On demand and accessible via web browser

Free Access for Packt account holders

If you have an account with Packt at www.PacktPub.com, you can use this to access PacktLib today and view nine entirely free books. Simply use your login credentials for immediate access.

Table of Contents

Preface

This book will show you how to use OpenCV's Java bindings in an Android app that displays a camera feed, saves and shares photos, manipulates colors and edges, and tracks real-world objects in 2D or 3D. Integration with OpenGL is also introduced so that you can start building augmented reality (AR) apps that superimpose virtual 3D scenes on tracked objects in the camera feed.

OpenCV is an open-source, cross-platform library that provides building blocks for computer vision experiments and applications. It offers high-level interfaces for capturing, processing, and presenting image data. For example, it abstracts away details about camera hardware and array allocation. OpenCV is widely used in both academia and industry.

Android is a mobile operating system that is mostly open source. For Java developers, it offers a high-level application framework called Android SDK. Android apps are modular insofar as they have standard, high-level interfaces for launching each other and sharing data. Mobility, a high level of abstraction, and data sharing are great starting points for a photo sharing app, similar to the one we will build.

Although OpenCV and Android provide a lot of high-level abstractions (and a lot of open source code for curious users to browse), they are not necessarily easy for newcomers. Setting up an appropriate development environment and translating the libraries' broad functionality into app features are both daunting tasks. This concise book helps by placing an emphasis on clean setup, clean application design, and a simple understanding of each function's purpose.

The need for a book on this subject is particularly great because the OpenCV's Java and Android bindings are quite new and their documentation is not yet mature. Little has been written about the steps for integrating OpenCV with an Android's standard camera, media, and graphics APIs. Surely integration is a major part of an app developer's work, so it is a major focus of this book.

By the end of our journey together, you will have a taste of the breadth of application features that are made possible by integrating OpenCV with other Android libraries. You will have your own small library of reusable classes that you can extend or modify for your future computer vision projects. You will have a development environment and the knowledge to use it, and you will be able to make more apps!

What this book covers

Chapter 1, Setting Up OpenCV, covers the steps to setting up OpenCV and an Android development environment, including Eclipse and Android SDK.

Chapter 2, Working with Camera Frames, shows how to integrate OpenCV into an Android app that can preview, capture, save, and share photos.

Chapter 3, Applying Image Effects, explores the OpenCV's functionality for manipulating color channels and neighborhoods of pixels. We expand our app to include channel-mixing filters, "curve" filters, and a filter that darkens edges.

Chapter 4, Recognizing and Tracking Images, demonstrates the steps to recognizing and tracking a known target (such as a painting) when it appears in a video feed. We expand our app so that it draws an outline around any tracked target.

Chapter 5, Combining Image Tracking with 3D Rendering, improves upon our previous tracking technique by determining the target's position and rotation in real 3D space. We expand our app so that it sets up an OpenGL 3D scene with the same perspective as the Android device's real camera. Then, we draw a 3D cube atop any tracked target.

What you need for this book

This book provides setup instructions for OpenCV and an Android development environment, including Eclipse and Android SDK. The software is cross platform and the instructions cover Windows, Mac, and Linux. Other Unix-like environments may work, too, if you are willing to do your own tailoring of the setup steps.

You need a mobile device running Android 2.2 (Froyo) or greater and it must have a camera. Preferably, it should have two cameras, front and rear. Also, it should preferably come with the Google Play Store app because OpenCV uses Google Play Store to manage installation and upgrades of shared libraries.

Who this book is for

This book is great for Java developers who are new to computer vision and who like to learn through application development. It is assumed that you have previous experience in Java but not necessarily Android. A basic understanding of image data (for example, pixels, color channels) would be helpful, too.

Conventions

In this book, you will find a number of styles of text that distinguish between different kinds of information. Here are some examples of these styles, and an explanation of their meaning.

Code words in text are shown as follows: "Edit your system's PATH to include `<android_sdk>/platform-tools` and `<android_sdk>/tools`."

A block of code is set as follows:

```
<?xml version="1.0" encoding="utf-8"?>
<manifest xmlns:android=
  "http://schemas.android.com/apk/res/android"
  package="com.nummist.secondsight"
  android:versionCode="1"
  android:versionName="1.0">
```

When we wish to draw your attention to a particular part of a code block, the relevant lines or items are set in bold:

```
mCameraView.enableView();
    mBgr = new Mat();
    mCurveFilters = new Filter[] {
      new NoneFilter(),
      new PortraCurveFilter(),
      new ProviaCurveFilter(),
```

Any command-line input or output is written as follows:

```
$ cd /etc/udev/rules.d/
$ sudo touch 51-android.rules
$ sudo chmod a+r 51-android-rules
```

New terms and **important words** are shown in bold. Words that you see on the screen, in menus or dialog boxes for example, appear in the text like this: "clicking on the **Next** button moves you to the next screen".

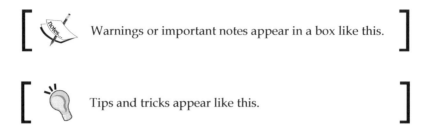

Warnings or important notes appear in a box like this.

Tips and tricks appear like this.

Reader feedback

Feedback from our readers is always welcome. Let us know what you think about this book—what you liked or may have disliked. Reader feedback is important for us to develop titles that you really get the most out of.

To send us general feedback, simply send an e-mail to feedback@packtpub.com, and mention the book title via the subject of your message.

If there is a topic that you have expertise in and you are interested in either writing or contributing to a book, see our author guide on www.packtpub.com/authors.

Customer support

Now that you are the proud owner of a Packt book, we have a number of things to help you to get the most from your purchase.

Downloading the example code

You can download the example code files for all Packt books you have purchased from your account at http://www.packtpub.com. If you purchased this book elsewhere, you can visit http://www.packtpub.com/support and register to have the files e-mailed directly to you. The example code for this book is also available from the author's website at http://nummist.com/opencv/.

Errata

Although we have taken every care to ensure the accuracy of our content, mistakes do happen. If you find a mistake in one of our books—maybe a mistake in the text or the code—we would be grateful if you would report this to us. By doing so, you can save other readers from frustration and help us improve subsequent versions of this book. If you find any errata, please report them by visiting http://www.packtpub.com/submit-errata, selecting your book, clicking on the **errata submission form** link, and entering the details of your errata. Once your errata are verified, your submission will be accepted and the errata will be uploaded on our website, or added to any list of existing errata, under the Errata section of that title. Any existing errata can be viewed by selecting your title from http://www.packtpub.com/support.

Piracy

Piracy of copyright material on the Internet is an ongoing problem across all media. At Packt, we take the protection of our copyright and licenses very seriously. If you come across any illegal copies of our works, in any form, on the Internet, please provide us with the location address or website name immediately so that we can pursue a remedy.

Please contact us at copyright@packtpub.com with a link to the suspected pirated material.

We appreciate your help in protecting our authors, and our ability to bring you valuable content.

Questions

You can contact us at questions@packtpub.com if you are having a problem with any aspect of the book, and we will do our best to address it. You can also contact the author directly at josephhowse@nummist.com or you can check his website, http://nummist.com/opencv/, for answers to common questions about this book.

Setting Up OpenCV

1

This chapter is a quick guide for setting up a development environment for Android and OpenCV. We will also look at the OpenCV sample applications, documentation, and community.

By the end of this chapter, our development environment will include the following components:

- **Java Development Kit (JDK) 6**: It includes tools for Java programming.
- **Cygwin 1.7 or greater (Windows only)**: It is a compatibility layer that provides Unix-like programming tools on Windows.
- **Android Software Development Kit (Android SDK) r21.0.1 or greater**: It includes tools for programming Android apps in Java.
- **Android Native Development Kit (Android NDK) r8d or greater**: It includes tools for programming Android apps in C++. Although this book deals with Java programming, OpenCV also includes Android-compatible C++ samples that you may want to compile and run.
- **Eclipse 4.2.1 (Juno) or greater**: It is an **integrated development environment (IDE)**.
- **Java Development Tools (JDT)**: It is an Eclipse plugin for Java programming (already included in most Eclipse distributions).
- **C/C++ Development Tooling (CDT) 8.1.1 or greater**: It is an Eclipse plugin for C/C++ programming.
- **Android Development Tools (ADT) 21.0.1 or greater**: It is an Eclipse plugin for Android programming.
- **OpenCV4Android 2.4.3.2 or greater**: It includes OpenCV's Android version, including Java and C++ libraries.

There are many possible ways to install and configure these components. We will cover several common setup scenarios, but if you are interested in even more options, see OpenCV's official documentation at `http://docs.opencv.org/doc/tutorials/introduction/android_binary_package/O4A_SDK.html`.

System requirements

All of the development tools for Android and OpenCV are cross platform. The following operating systems are supported with almost identical setup procedures:

- Windows XP, Windows Vista, Windows 7, or Windows 8
- Mac OS 10.6 (Snow Leopard) or greater
- Ubuntu 10.10 (Maverick) or greater
- Many other Unix-like systems (though not specifically covered in this book)

To run the OpenCV samples and, later, our own application, we should have an Android device with the following specifications:

- Android 2.2 (Froyo) or greater (required)
- Camera (required); front and rear cameras (recommended)
- Autofocus (recommended)
- Google Play Store (recommended)

Android Virtual Devices (**AVDs**) are not recommended. Some parts of OpenCV rely on low-level camera access and may fail with virtualized cameras.

Setting up a development environment

Basically, we have a choice among the following approaches:

1. Install a prepackaged, preconfigured development environment that contains all the components we need.
2. Install various components separately and configure them to work together. Within this approach, we may do either of the following:
    - Use a prepackaged, preconfigured version of OpenCV
    - Configure and build OpenCV from source

Let's look at each of these alternatives in detail.

Getting a ready-made development environment – Tegra Android Development Pack (TAPD)

Tegra Android Development Pack (**TADP**) contains a complete, preconfigured development environment for Android, OpenCV, and some other libraries. TADP builds apps that are optimized for NVIDIA's Tegra processors. Despite being optimized for Tegra, the apps are compatible with other hardware too.

> If you are setting up an Android development environment from scratch, I recommend TADP. It contains recent versions of all our required software and its setup process is simple.
>
> TADP also contains some extras that we do not require for this book. For a complete list of TADP's contents, see the official description at https://developer.nvidia.com/tegra-android-development-pack.

To set up TADP, we just need to download and install it from a secure section of NVIDIA's website. Here are the required steps:

1. Join the NVIDIA Registered Developer Program at https://developer.nvidia.com/user/register. (It is free.)

2. Log in at https://developer.nvidia.com/user/login.

3. Complete your user profile at https://developer.nvidia.com/user/me/profile/rdp_profile.

4. Apply to join the Tegra Registered Developer Program at https://developer.nvidia.com/rdp/applications/tegra-registered-developer-program. (It is free, too!) Wait for NVIDIA to send you an acceptance email. Normally, you might receive it a few minutes after applying.

5. Go to https://developer.nvidia.com/tegra-resources and find the download link for TADP's latest version. At the time of writing, the latest version is 2.0r2. There are installers for Windows (32-bit or 64-bit), Mac, and Ubuntu (32-bit or 64-bit). Download and run the appropriate installer.

6. When the installer presents the **Installation Directory** step, we can enter any destination, which we will refer to as <tadp>. By default, <tadp> is C:\NVPACK (Windows) or ~/NVPACK (Mac and Ubuntu).

7. When the installer presents the **Installation Options** step, we may select any option: **Complete**, **Express**, or **Custom**. Compared to an **Express** installation, a **Complete** or **Custom** installation may include additional versions of Android SDK and binary images of Tegra Android OS, which is NVIDIA's customization of Android. If in doubt, choose **Express**.

8. When the installer presents the **Proxy Configuration** step, we may leave all fields blank unless we are using a proxy server.

9. After finishing all of the installer's configuration steps, wait for TADP's content to be downloaded and installed.

That's all! Before proceeding, let's just take a note of the locations where TADP has installed certain components. For TADP 2.0r2 (the latest version at the time of writing), the locations are as follows:

- Android SDK is located at `<tadp>/android-sdk-macosx`. We will refer to this location as `<android_sdk>`.

- Android NDK is located at `<tadp>/android-ndk-r8d`. We will refer to this location as `<android_ndk>`.

- OpenCV4Android is located at `<tadp>/OpenCV-2.4.3.2-android-sdk-tadp`. We will refer to this location as `<opencv>`.

- Eclipse is located at `<tadp>/eclipse`. We will refer to this location as `<eclipse>`.

> The TADP installer automatically edits the system's PATH to include `<android_sdk>/platform-tools` and `<android_sdk>/tools`. Also, it creates an environment variable called NDKROOT, whose value is `<android_ndk>`.

Now, we can proceed to *Building the OpenCV Samples with Eclipse*, later in this chapter.

Downloading the example code

You can download the example code files for all Packt books you have purchased from your account at http://www.packtpub.com. If you purchased this book elsewhere, you can visit http://www.packtpub.com/support and register to have the files e-mailed directly to you. The example code for this book is also available from the author's website at http://nummist.com/opencv/.

Assembling a development environment piece-by-piece

Instead of using TADP as a ready-made solution, we may assemble our own development environment. Broadly, this task has two stages:

- Set up a general-purpose Android development environment
- Set up OpenCV for use in this environment

Let's start by looking at the setup steps for a general-purpose Android development environment. We will not delve into very much detail here, because good instructions are available at the given links and, because you, as an Android developer, have probably been through similar steps before.

 If you already have an Android development environment and you just want to add components to it, some of the following steps will not apply to you.

Here are the steps:

1. If we are using Windows or Linux, we may need to obtain JDK 6 manually. (On Mac, if JDK 6 is not present, the operating system will automatically offer to install it when needed.) The JDK 6 installers or packages are available for Windows and many Linux distributions at `http://www.oracle.com/technetwork/java/javase/downloads/jdk6downloads-1902814.html`. Alternatively, on Linux, check your repository for the JDK packages. Install JDK 6.

2. Download Eclipse and unzip it to any destination, which we will refer to as `<eclipse>`. There are many versions from which we may choose. Google provides an Eclipse distribution called **Android Developer Tools (ADT) Bundle**, which comes with Android SDK and the ADT plugin prepackaged and preconfigured. ADT Bundle is available at `http://developer.android.com/sdk/index.html`. Many other up-to-date Eclipse distributions are available at `http://www.eclipse.org/downloads/`. Of these, Eclipse for Mobile Developers is a good and minimalist choice as a foundation for an Android development environment.

3. If we did not get the ADT Bundle, we now need to set up Android SDK and the ADT plugin for Eclipse. Go to `http://developer.android.com/sdk/index.html` and get the download named Android SDK Tools. Install or unzip it to any destination, which we will refer to as `<android_sdk>`. Open Eclipse and install the ADT plugin according to the official instructions at `http://developer.android.com/sdk/installing/installing-adt.html`. Restart Eclipse. A window, **Welcome to Android Development**, should appear. Click on **Use Existing SDKs**, browse to `<android_sdk>`, and click on **Next**. Close Eclipse.

4. If we are using Windows, download and install Cygwin from `http://cygwin.com/install.html`.

5. Download Android NDK from `http://developer.android.com/tools/sdk/ndk/index.html`. Unzip it to any destination, which we will refer to as `<android_ndk>`.

6. Edit your system's PATH to include `<android_sdk>/platform-tools` and `<android_sdk>/tools`. Also, create an environment variable named NDKROOT with the value as `<android_ndk>`. (If you are unsure how to edit PATH and other environment variables, see *Appendix A: Editing environment variables*.)

Editing environment variables on Windows

The system's `Path` variable and other environment variables can be edited in the **Environment Variables** window of **Control Panel**.

On Windows Vista/7/8, open the **Start** menu and launch **Control Panel**. Now, go to **System and Security** | **System** | **Advanced system settings**. Click on the **Environment Variables** button.

On Windows XP, open the Start menu and go to **Control Panel** | **System**. Click on the **Advanced** tab. Click on the **Environment Variables** button.

Now, under **System variables**, select an existing environment variable, such as `Path`, and click on the **Edit** button. Alternatively, make a new environment variable by clicking on the **New** button. Edit the variable's name and value as needed. For example, if we want to add `C:\android-sdk\platform-tools` and `C:\android-sdk\tools` to `Path`, we should append `;C:\android-sdk\platform-tools;C:\android-sdk\tools` to the existing value of `Path`. Note the use of semicolons as separators.

To apply the changes, click on all the **OK** buttons until we are back in the main window of Control Panel. Now, log out and again log in.

Editing environment variables on Mac

Edit `~/.profile`.

To append to an existing environment variable, add a line such as `export PATH=$PATH:~/android-sdk/platform-tools:~/android-sdk/tools`. This example appends `~/android-sdk/platform-tools` and `~/android-sdk/tools` to `PATH`. Note the use of colons as separators.

To create a new environment variable, add a line such as `export NDKROOT=~/android-ndk`.

Save your changes, log out, and again log in.

Editing environment variables on Ubuntu

Edit `~/.pam_environment`.

To append to an existing environment variable, add a line such as `PATH DEFAULT=${PATH}:~/android-sdk/platform-tools:~/android-sdk/tools`. This example appends `~/android-sdk/platform-tools` and `~/android-sdk/tools` to `PATH`. Note the use of colons as separators.

To create a new environment variable, add a line such as `NDKROOT DEFAULT=~/android-ndk`.

Save your changes, log out, and again log in.

Now, we have an Android development environment but we still need OpenCV. We may choose to download a prebuilt version of OpenCV or we may build it from source. These options are discussed in the following two subsections.

Generally, Android applications should use a prebuilt version of OpenCV. One important reason is that the prebuilt versions are available for Android users as shared libraries, which save disk space and simplify updates.

For the purpose of this book's project, there is no need to build OpenCV from source. We just mention this option for completeness, since it may be of interest to advanced users who want to modify OpenCV.

Getting the prebuilt OpenCV4Android

The prebuilt versions of OpenCV4Android can be downloaded from `http://sourceforge.net/projects/opencvlibrary/files/opencv-android/`. Look for files that have `opencv-android` in the name, such as `OpenCV-2.4.5-android-sdk.zip` (the latest version at the time of writing). Download the latest version and unzip it to any destination, which we will refer to as `<opencv>`.

Building OpenCV4Android from source

Alternatively, the process for building OpenCV4Android from **trunk** (the latest, unstable source code) is documented at `http://code.opencv.org/projects/opencv/wiki/Building_OpenCV4Android_from_trunk`. For a summary of the process for building from trunk, continue reading this section. Otherwise, skip ahead to *Building the OpenCV samples with Eclipse*, later in this chapter.

Since trunk contains the latest and unstable source code, there is no guarantee that the build process will succeed. You may need to do your own troubleshooting if you want to build from trunk.

To build OpenCV from source, we need the following additional software:

- **Git**: It is a **Source Control Management (SCM)** tool, which we will use to obtain OpenCV's source code. On Windows or Mac, download and install Git from `http://git-scm.com/`. On Linux, install it using your package manager. For example, on Ubuntu, open Terminal and run `$ sudo apt-get install git-core`.

- **CMake**: It is a set of build tools. On Windows or Mac, download and install CMake from `http://www.cmake.org/cmake/resources/software.html`. On Linux, install it using your package manager. For example, on Ubuntu, open Terminal and run `$ sudo apt-get install cmake`.

- **Apache Ant 1.8.0 or greater**: It is a set of build tools for Java. On Linux, just install Ant using your package manager. For example, on Ubuntu, open Terminal and run `$ sudo apt-get install ant`. On Windows or Mac, download Ant from `http://ant.apache.org/bindownload.cgi` and unzip it to any destination, which we will refer to as `<ant>`. Make the following changes to your environment variables:
  - ○ Add `<ant>/bin` to `PATH`.
  - ○ Create a variable, `ANT_HOME`, with the value `<ant>`.

- **Python 2.6 or greater (but not 3.0 or greater)**: It is a scripting language that is used by some of the OpenCV build scripts. An appropriate version of Python comes preinstalled on Mac and most Linux systems, including Ubuntu. On Windows, download and install Python from `http://www.python.org/getit/`. If you have installed multiple versions of Python on your system, ensure that an installation of Python 2.6 or greater (but not 3.0 or greater) is the only one in `Path` (Windows) or `PATH` (Mac, Linux, or other Unix-like systems). The OpenCV build scripts do not run properly with Python 3.0 or greater.

Once we have these prerequisites, we may download the OpenCV source code to any location, which we will refer to as `<opencv_source>`. Then, we may build it using an included script. The steps are platform-specific, and are described as follows:

On Windows, copy `<opencv>\android\scripts\wincfg.cmd.tmpl` to `<opencv>\android\scripts\wincfg.cmd`. Edit `<opencv>\android\scripts\wincfg.cmd`. The locations of several of the prerequisites are declared in this file. Modify them so that they are correct for your system. Save your changes. Then, open Git Bash (Git's command prompt) and run the following commands:

```
$ git clone git://code.opencv.org/opencv.git <opencv_source>
$ cd <opencv_source>/android
$ scripts/cmake_android.cmd
$ cd build
$ make -j8
```

On Mac, Ubuntu, or other Unix-like systems, open Terminal (or another command line shell) and run the following commands:

```
$ git clone git://code.opencv.org/opencv.git <opencv_source>
$ cd <opencv_source>/android
$ sh ./scripts/cmake_android.sh
$ cd build
$ make -j8
```

If all goes well, we should get a build of OpenCV4Android in <opencv_source>/android/build. We may move it elsewhere if we wish. We will refer to its final location as <opencv>.

Building the OpenCV samples with Eclipse

Building and running a few sample applications is a good way to test that OpenCV is correctly set up. At the same time, we can practice using Eclipse.

Let's start by launching Eclipse. The Eclipse launcher should be located at <eclipse>/eclipse.exe (Windows), <eclipse>/Eclipse.app (Mac), or <eclipse>/eclipse (Linux). Run it.

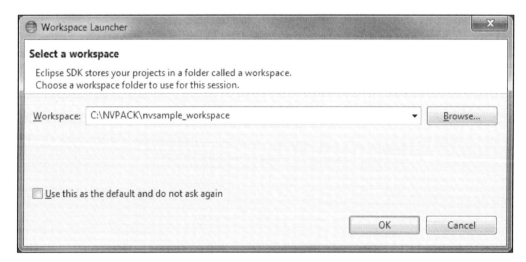

We should see a window called **Workspace Launcher**, which asks us to select a workspace. A **workspace** is the root directory for a set of related Eclipse projects. If we are using TADP, enter `<tadp>/nvsample_workspace`, which is a workspace where the OpenCV4Android library, samples, and tutorials are already set up as projects. Otherwise, enter any location you choose.

 We can return to **Workspace Launcher** anytime via the menu: **File | Switch Workspace | Other...**.

If the **Welcome to Eclipse** screen appears, click on the **Workbench** button.

Now, we should see a window with several panels, including **Package Explorer**. If we are not using TAPD, we need to import the OpenCV sample projects into our new workspace. Right-click on **Package Explorer** and select **Import…** from the context menu.

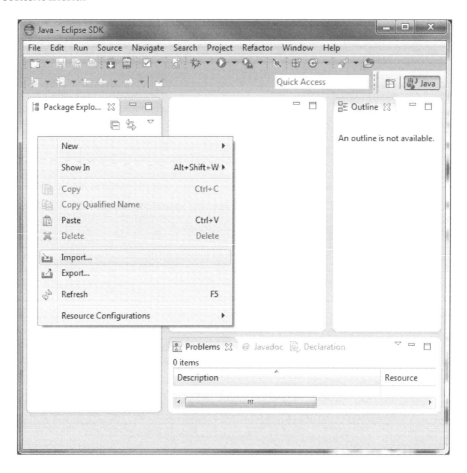

The **Import** window should appear. Select **General | Existing Projects into Workspace**, and then click on **Next>**.

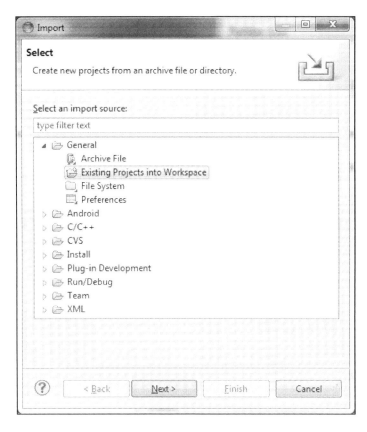

On the second page of the **Import** window, enter <opencv> in the **Select root directory:** field. Under the **Projects:** label, a list of detected projects should appear (If not, click on **Refresh**). The list should include OpenCV library, samples, and tutorials. Ensure that all projects are selected and click on **Finish** to import them.

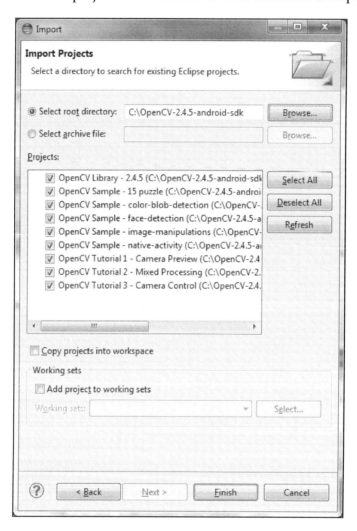

Once the projects are imported, we may need to fix some configuration issues. Our development environment may have different paths, and different versions of the Android SDK, than the ones in the samples' default configuration.

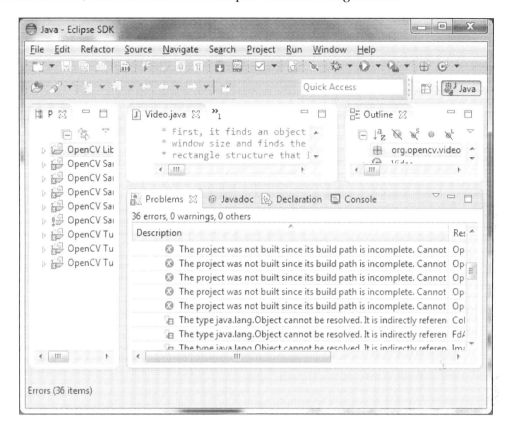

Any resulting errors will be reported in the **Problems** tab.

We should start by resolving any errors in the **OpenCV Library** project, as the samples and tutorials depend on the library.

The following are some of the common configuration problems, and their symptoms and solutions:

- The target Android version might not be properly specified. The symptoms are that imports from the java and android packages fail, and there are error messages such as `The project was not built since its build path is incomplete`. The solution is to right-click on the project in **Package Explorer**, select **Properties** from the context menu, select the **Android** section, and checkmark one of the available Android versions. These steps should be repeated for all projects. At compile time, OpenCV and its samples must target Android 3.0 (API level 11) or greater, though at runtime they also support Android 2.2 (API level 8) or greater.

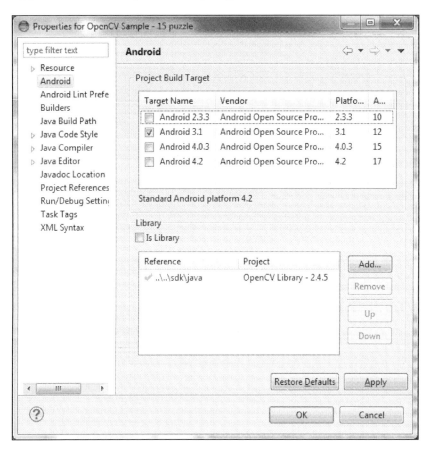

- If we are working on Mac or Linux, the C++ samples might be misconfigured to use the Windows build executable. The symptom is an error message such as `Program "{ndk}/ndk-build.cmd" not found in PATH`. The solution is to right-click on the project in **Package Explorer**, select **Properties** from the context menu, select the **C/C++ Build** section, and edit the **Build command:** field to remove the `.cmd` extension. These steps should be repeated for all the native (C++) projects, which include **OpenCV Sample - face-detection and OpenCV Tutorial 2 - Mixed Processing**.

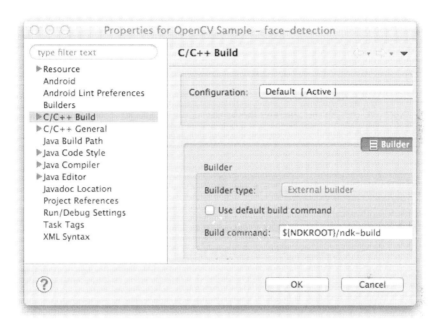

 If we are using the projects in TADP's `<tadp>/nvsample_workspace`, we only need to troubleshoot the projects that have names starting with `OpenCV`. For this book's purposes, the other TADP samples are not relevant.

Once the OpenCV projects no longer show any errors, we can prepare to test them on an Android device. Recall that the device must have Android 2.2 (Froyo) or a greater version, and a camera. To enable Eclipse to communicate with the device, we must enable the device's USB debugging option with the help of the following steps:

1. Open the Settings app.

2. On Android 4.2 or greater, go to the **About phone** or **About tablet** section and tap **Build number** seven times. This step enables the **Developer options** section.

3. Go to the **Developer options** section (on Android 4.0 or greater) or the **Applications | Development** section (on Android 3.2 or less). Enable the **USB debugging** option.

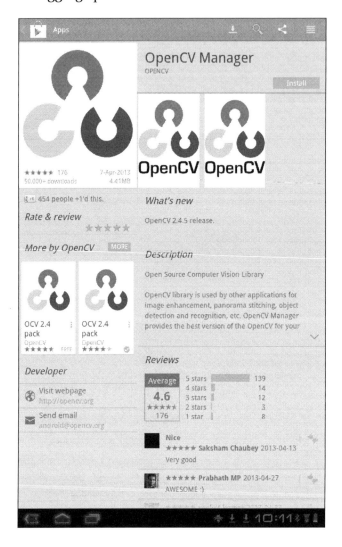

Now, open the Play Store app, and find and install the **OpenCV Manager** app. (The app's page in the Play Store should look similar to the previous screenshot.) OpenCV Manager takes care of checking for any OpenCV library updates when we run any OpenCV applications.

If you do not have the Play Store app on your device, then you need to install OpenCV Manager and certain OpenCV libraries via USB as per the instructions at `http://docs.opencv.org/android/service/doc/UseCases.html`.

Now, we must prepare our main computer for communication with the Android device. The required steps vary, depending on our operating system.

On Windows, we need to install the proper USB drivers for the Android device. Different vendors and devices have different drivers. The official Android documentation provides links to the various vendors' driver download sites at `http://developer.android.com/tools/extras/oem-usb.html#Drivers`.

On Linux, before connecting an Android device via USB, we must specify the device's vendor in a permissions file. Each vendor has a unique ID number, as listed in the official Android documentation at `http://developer.android.com/tools/device.html#VendorIds`. We will refer to this ID number as `<vendor_id>`. To create the permissions file, open a command prompt application (such as Terminal) and run the following commands:

```
$ cd /etc/udev/rules.d/
$ sudo touch 51-android.rules
$ sudo chmod a+r 51-android-rules
```

Note that the permissions file needs to have root ownership, so we use `sudo` when creating or modifying it. Now, open the file in an editor such as gedit:

```
$ sudo gedit 51-android-rules
```

For each vendor, append a new line to the file. Each of these lines should have the following format:

```
SUBSYSTEM=="usb", ATTR{idVendor}=="<vendor_id>", MODE="0666",
GROUP="plugdev"
```

Save the permissions file and quit the editor.

On Mac, no special drivers or permissions are required.

Plug the Android device into your computer's USB port. In Eclipse, select one of the OpenCV sample projects in **Package Explorer**. Then, from the menu system, select **Run | Run as… | Android Application**.

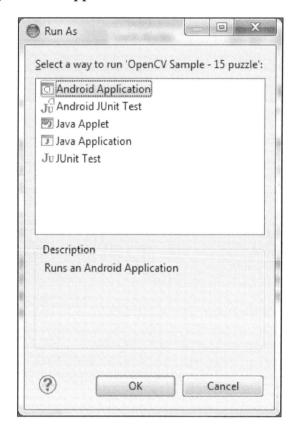

An **Android Device Chooser** window should appear. Your Android device should be listed under **Choose a running Android device**. (If the device is not listed, try unplugging it and plugging it back in. If that does not work, also try disabling and re-enabling the device's **USB debugging** option, as described earlier.)

Select the device and click on **OK**.

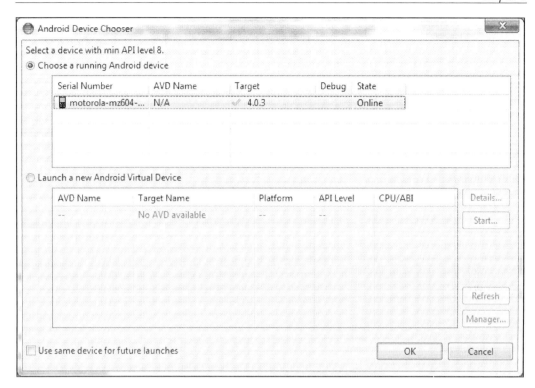

If the **Auto Monitor Logcat** window appears, select the **Yes** radio button and the **verbose** drop-down option, and click on **OK**. This option ensures that all the log output from the application will be visible in Eclipse.

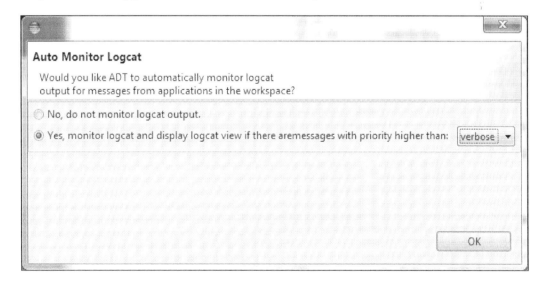

On the Android device you might get a message: **OpenCV library package was not found! Try to install it?** Make sure the device is connected to the Internet and then touch the **Yes** button on your device. The Play Store will open to show an OpenCV package. Install the package and then press the hardware back button to return to the sample application, which should be ready for use.

For OpenCV 2.4.3.2, the samples and tutorials have the following functionality:

- **Sample – 15 puzzle**: It splits up a camera feed to make a sliding-block puzzle. The user may swipe blocks to move them.

- **Sample – color-blob-detection**: It detects color regions in a camera feed. The user may touch anywhere to see the outline of a color region.

- **Sample – face-detection**: It draws green rectangles around faces in a camera feed.

- **Sample – image-manipulations**: It applies filters to a camera feed. The user may press the Android menu button to select from a list of filters.

- **Tutorial 1 – Add OpenCV**: It displays a camera feed. The user may press the ... menu to select a different camera feed implementation (Java or native C++).

- **Tutorial 2 – Use OpenCV Camera**: It applies filters to a camera feed. The user may press the ... menu to select from a list of filters.

- **Tutorial 3 – Add Native OpenCV**: It draws red circles around interest points or features in a camera feed. Generally speaking, interest points or features lie along the high-contrast edges in an image. They are potentially useful in image recognition and tracking applications.

- **Tutorial 4 – Mix Java+Native OpenCV**: It combines the functionality of Tutorial 2 and Tutorial 3. The user may press the ... menu to select from a list of filters and a preview of interest points.

- **Tutorial 5 – Camera Control**: It applies filters to a camera feed, which has a customizable resolution. The user may press the ... menu to select from a list of filters and a list of resolutions.

Try these applications on your Android device! While an application is running, its log output should appear in the **LogCat** tab in Eclipse.

Feel free to browse the projects' source code via **Package Explorer**, to see how they were made. Alternatively, you might want to return to the official samples and tutorials later, after we have built our own project over the course of this book.

Finding documentation and help

The OpenCV Java API and C++ API are both relevant to Android. The Java API documentation is online at http://docs.opencv.org/java/. The C++ API documentation is online at http://docs.opencv.org/. The following documents, which mostly use C++ code, are also available as downloadable PDF files:

- API reference: http://docs.opencv.org/opencv2refman.pdf
- Tutorials: http://docs.opencv.org/opencv_tutorials.pdf
- User guide (incomplete): http://docs.opencv.org/opencv_user.pdf

If the documentation does not seem to answer your question, try talking to the OpenCV community. Here are some sites where you will find helpful people:

- Official OpenCV forum: http://www.answers.opencv.org/questions/
- Jay Rambhia's blog: http://jayrambhia.wordpress.com/
- The support site for my OpenCV books: http://nummist.com/opencv/

Also, you can read or submit bug reports at http://code.opencv.org/projects/opencv/issues?query_id=4. Finally, if you need to take your issue to the highest authority, you can email the OpenCV4Android developers at android@opencv.org.

Summary

By now, we should have an Android and OpenCV development environment that can do everything we need for the project described in this book. Depending on which approach we took, we might also have a set of tools that we can use to reconfigure and rebuild OpenCV for our future needs.

We know how to build the OpenCV Android samples in Eclipse. These samples cover a different range of functionality than this book's project, but they are useful as additional learning aids. We also know where to find documentation and help.

2
Working with Camera Frames

In this chapter, we focus on building a basic photo capture app, which uses OpenCV to capture frames of camera input. Our app will enable the user to preview, save, edit, and share photos. It will interface with other apps on the device, via Android's `MediaStore` and `Intent` classes. Thus, we will learn how to build bridges between OpenCV and standard Android. Subsequent chapters will expand our app, using more functionality from OpenCV.

> The complete Eclipse project for this chapter can be downloaded from my website, `http://nummist.com/opencv/5206_02.zip`.

Designing our app – Second Sight

Let's make an app that enables people to see new visual patterns, to animate and interact with these patterns, and to share them as pictures. The idea is simple and versatile. Anyone, from a child to a computer vision expert, can appreciate the patterns. Through the magic of computer vision on a mobile device, any user can more readily see, change, and share hidden patterns in any scene.

For this app, I chose the name `Second Sight`, a phrase that is sometimes used in mythology to refer to supernatural and symbolic visions.

At its core, `Second Sight` is a camera app. It will enable the user to preview, save, and share photos. Like many other camera apps, it will also let the user to apply filters to the preview and the saved photos. However, many of the filters will not be traditional photographic effects. For example, the more complex filters will enable the user to see stylized edges or even rendered objects that blend with the real scene (**augmented reality**).

For this chapter, we will just build the basic camera and sharing functions of Second Sight, without any filters. Our first version of the app will contain two activity classes named CameraActivity and LabActivity. The CameraActivity class will show the preview and provide menu actions so that the user may select a camera (if the device has multiple cameras) and take a photo. Then, the LabActivity class will open to show the saved photo and will provide menu actions so that the user may delete the photo, or send it to another app for editing or sharing.

To get a better sense of our goal, let's look at some screenshots. Our first version of CameraActivity will look as follows:

When the user presses the **Take Photo** menu item, the LabActivity class will open. It will look like the following screenshot:

When the user presses the **Share** menu item, an intent chooser (a dialog for choosing a destination app) will appear overtop the photo, as in the following screenshot:

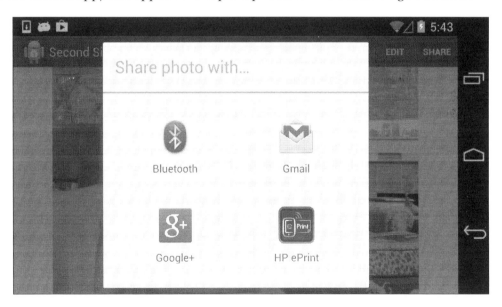

For example, by pressing the **Google+** tile, the user could open the photo in the Google+ app, in order to share it over the social network. Thus, we have a complete usage example, where the user can snap a photo and share it, using just a few touch interactions.

Creating the Eclipse project

We need to create a new Eclipse project for our app. We may do this in the same workspace that we already used for the OpenCV library project and samples. Alternatively, if we use another workspace, we must import the OpenCV library project into this workspace too. (For instructions on setting the workspace and importing the library project, see the *Building the OpenCV samples with Eclipse* section of *Chapter 1, Setting Up OpenCV*.)

Open Eclipse to a workspace that contains the library project. Then, from the menu system, navigate to **File | New | Android Application Project**. The **New Android Application** window should appear. Enter the options that are shown in the following screenshot:

The **Target SDK** and **Compile With** fields should be set to API 11 (Android 3.0) or higher. It is safe to choose the most recent API version, which, at the time of writing, is **API 17: Android 4.2 (Jelly Bean)**. The **Minimum Required SDK** field should be left at the default, **API 8: Android 2.2 (Froyo)**, because we will write fallbacks to enable our code to run on that version.

Click on the **Next** button. A checklist should appear. Ensure that the only checked options are **Create activity** and **Create Project in Workspace**, as in the following screenshot:

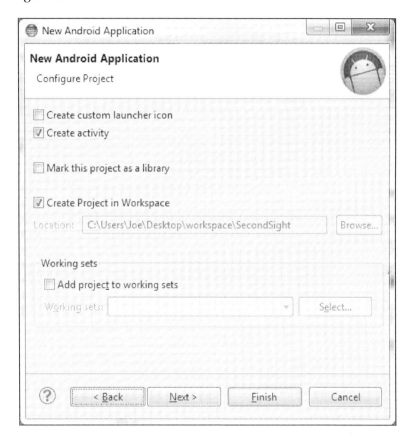

Click on the **Next** button. A list of activity templates should appear. Select **BlankActivity**, as in the following screenshot:

Click on the **Next** button. More options about the activity should appear. Enter CameraActivity in the **Activity Name** field, as in the following screenshot:

Click on the **Finish** button. Our project is created. We should be able to browse its contents in the **Package Explorer** pane. Let's remove and add some files, according to the following steps:

1. Delete `res/layout/activity_camera.xml`. (Right-click on it, select **Delete** from the context menu and click on **OK**.) The layout of our interface will be very simple, so it will be more convenient to create it in Java code instead of this separate XML file. However, if you do want an example of using OpenCV with an XML layout, you may refer to the sample apps that come with the library. See the *Building the OpenCV samples with Eclipse* section in *Chapter 1*, *Setting Up OpenCV*.

2. Create `src/com/nummist/secondsight/LabActivity.java`. (Right-click on **com.nummist.secondsight**, navigate to **New | Class** from the context menu, enter `LabActivity` in the **Name** field, and click on **Finish**.)

3. Create `res/menu/activity_lab.xml`. (Right-click on the parent folder, navigate to **New | Android XML File** from the context menu, enter `activity_lab` in the **File** field, and click on **Finish**.)

Now, we have the skeleton of our project. Throughout the rest of this chapter, we will edit several files to provide appropriate functionality and content.

Enabling camera and disk access in the manifest

The AndroidManifest.xml (the **manifest**) file specifies an Android app's requirements and components. Compared to the default manifest, the manifest in Second Sight needs to do the following additional work:

- Ensure that the device has at least one camera.

- Get permission to use the camera.

- Get permission to write the files to the permanent storage.

- Restrict the screen orientation to landscape mode because OpenCV's camera preview does not handle portrait mode well. For more description over the issue and some attempted workarounds, see the StackOverflow thread at http://answers.opencv.org/question/7143/mirror-image-on-android-front-camera/. Also see the blog post by Yu Lu and the comments posted by her readers at http://littlecheesecake.wordpress.com/2012/03/12/display-orientation-issue-when-working-with-opencv-on-android/.

- Register the second activity.

We can accomplish these tasks by editing the uses-permission, uses-feature, and activity tags in the manifest.

 For details about the Android manifest, see the official documentation at http://developer.android.com/guide/topics/manifest/manifest-intro.html.

Open AndroidManifest.xml, which is under the project's root directory. View it in the source code mode by clicking on the tab labeled **AndroidManifest.xml**. Edit the file by adding the highlighted code in the following snippet:

```xml
<?xml version="1.0" encoding="utf-8"?>
<manifest xmlns:android=
  "http://schemas.android.com/apk/res/android"
  package="com.nummist.secondsight"
  android:versionCode="1"
  android:versionName="1.0">
```

```xml
<uses-sdk
  android:minSdkVersion="8"
  android:targetSdkVersion="17" />

<uses-permission android:name="android.permission.CAMERA" />
<uses-permission android:name=
  "android.permission.WRITE_EXTERNAL_STORAGE" />

<uses-feature android:name="android.hardware.camera" />
<uses-feature android:name="android.hardware.camera.autofocus"
  android:required="false" />
<uses-feature android:name="android.hardware.camera.flash"
  android:required="false" />

<application
  android:allowBackup="true"
  android:icon="@drawable/ic_launcher"
  android:label="@string/app_name"
  android:theme="@style/AppTheme">
  <activity
    android:name="com.nummist.secondsight.CameraActivity"
    android:label="@string/app_name"
    android:screenOrientation="landscape">
    <intent-filter>
      <action android:name="android.intent.action.MAIN" />
      <category android:name=
        "android.intent.category.LAUNCHER" />
    </intent-filter>
  </activity>
  <activity
    android:name="com.nummist.secondsight.LabActivity"
    android:label="@string/app_name"
    android:screenOrientation="landscape">
  </activity>
</application>
</manifest>
```

Creating menu and string resources

Our app's menus and localizable text are described in XML files. Identifiers in these resource files are referenced by Java code, as we will see later.

 For details about Android app resources, see the official documentation at http://developer.android.com/guide/topics/ resources/index.html.

First, let's edit res/menu/activity_camera.xml so that it has the following implementation, describing the menu items for CameraActivity:

```
<menu xmlns:android="http://schemas.android.com/apk/res/android" >
  <item
    android:id="@+id/menu_next_camera"
    android:orderInCategory="100"
    android:showAsAction="ifRoom|withText"
    android:title="@string/menu_next_camera"/>
  <item
    android:id="@+id/menu_take_photo"
    android:orderInCategory="100"
    android:showAsAction="always|withText"
    android:title="@string/menu_take_photo"/>
</menu>
```

Note that we use the android:showAsAction attribute to make menu items appear in the app's top bar, as seen in the earlier screenshots.

Similarly, the menu items for LabActivity are described in res/menu/activity_ lab.xml, as follows:

```
<menu xmlns:android="http://schemas.android.com/apk/res/android" >
  <item
    android:id="@+id/menu_delete"
    android:orderInCategory="100"
    android:showAsAction="ifRoom|withText"
    android:title="@string/delete" />
  <item
```

```
        android:id="@+id/menu_edit"
        android:orderInCategory="100"
        android:showAsAction="ifRoom|withText"
        android:title="@string/edit" />
    <item
        android:id="@+id/menu_share"
        android:orderInCategory="100"
        android:showAsAction="ifRoom|withText"
        android:title="@string/share" />
</menu>
```

Strings of user-readable text, used in various places in the app, are described in `res/values/strings.xml` as follows:

```
<?xml version="1.0" encoding="utf-8"?>
<resources>
    <string name="app_name">Second Sight</string>
    <string name="delete">Delete</string>
    <string name="edit">Edit</string>
    <string name="menu_next_camera">Next Cam</string>
    <string name="menu_take_photo">Take Photo</string>
    <string name="photo_delete_prompt_message">This photo is saved
        in your Gallery. Do you want to delete it?</string>
    <string name="photo_delete_prompt_title">Delete photo?</string>
    <string name="photo_error_message">Failed to save photo</string>
    <string name="photo_edit_chooser_title">Edit photo
        with&#8230;</string>
    <string name="photo_send_chooser_title">Share photo
        with&#8230;</string>
    <string name="photo_send_extra_subject">My photo from Second
        Sight</string>
    <string name="photo_send_extra_text">Check out my photo from the
        Second Sight app! http://nummist.com/opencv/</string>
    <string name="share">Share</string>
</resources>
```

Having defined these boilerplate resources, we can proceed to implementing our app's functionality in Java.

Previewing and saving photos in CameraActivity

Our main activity, `CameraActivity`, needs to do the following:

- On startup, use OpenCV Manager to ensure that the appropriate OpenCV shared libraries are available. (For more information about OpenCV Manager, refer back to the *Building the OpenCV samples with Eclipse* section in *Chapter 1, Setting Up OpenCV*.)
- Display a live camera feed.
- Provide the following menu actions:

    ○ Switch the active camera (for a device that has multiple cameras).
    ○ Save a photo and insert it into `MediaStore` so that it is accessible to apps such as `Gallery`. Immediately open the photo in `LabActivity`.

We will use OpenCV functionality wherever feasible, even though we could just use the standard Android libraries to display a live camera feed, save a photo, and so on.

OpenCV provides an abstract class called `CameraBridgeViewBase`, which represents a live camera feed. This class extends Android's `SurfaceView` class, so that its instances can be part of the view hierarchy. Moreover, a `CameraBridgeViewBase` instance can dispatch events to any listener that implements one of two interfaces, either `CvCameraViewListener` or `CvCameraViewListener2`. Often, the listener will be an activity, as is the case with `CameraActivity`.

The `CvCameraViewListener` and `CvCameraViewListener2` interfaces provide callbacks for handling the start and stop of a stream of camera input, and for handling the capture of each frame. The two interfaces differ in terms of the image format. `CvCameraViewListener` always receives an RGBA color frame, which is passed as an instance of OpenCV's `Mat` class, a multidimensional array that may store pixel data. `CvCameraViewListener2` receives each frame as an instance of OpenCV's `CvCameraViewFrame` class. From the passed `CvCameraViewFrame`, we may get a `Mat` image in either RGBA color or grayscale format. Thus, `CvCameraViewListener2` is the more flexible interface and it is the one we implement in `CameraActivity`.

Since `CameraBridgeViewBase` is an abstract class, we need an implementation. OpenCV provides two implementations, `JavaCameraView` and `NativeCameraView`. They are both Java classes but `NativeCameraView` is a Java wrapper around a native C++ class. `NativeCameraView` tends to yield a higher frame rate, so it is the implementation that we use in `CameraActivity`.

To support interaction between OpenCV Manager and client apps, OpenCV provides an abstract class called `BaseLoaderCallback`. This class declares a callback method that is executed after OpenCV Manager ensures that the library is available. Typically, this callback is the appropriate place to enable any other OpenCV objects such as the camera view.

Now that we know something about the relevant OpenCV types, let's open `CameraActivity.java`, and add the following declarations of our activity class and its member variables:

 For brevity, the code listings in this book omit `package` and `import` statements. Eclipse should auto-generate `package` statements when you create files and `import` statements when you declare variables.

```java
public class CameraActivity extends FragmentActivity
    implements CvCameraViewListener2 {

    // A tag for log output.
    private static final String TAG = "MainActivity";

    // A key for storing the index of the active camera.
    private static final String STATE_CAMERA_INDEX = "cameraIndex";

    // The index of the active camera.
    private int mCameraIndex;

    // Whether the active camera is front facing.
    // If so, the camera view should be mirrored.
    private boolean mIsCameraFrontFacing;

    // The number of cameras on the device.
    private int mNumCameras;

    // The camera view.
    private CameraBridgeViewBase mCameraView;

    // Whether the next camera frame should be saved as a photo.
    private boolean mIsPhotoPending;

    // A matrix that is used when saving photos.
    private Mat mBgr;
```

```
    // Whether an asynchronous menu action is in progress.
    // If so, menu interaction should be disabled.
    private boolean mIsMenuLocked;

    // The OpenCV loader callback.
    private BaseLoaderCallback mLoaderCallback =
      new BaseLoaderCallback(this) {
        @Override
      public void onManagerConnected(final int status) {
        switch (status) {
          case LoaderCallbackInterface.SUCCESS:
            Log.d(TAG, "OpenCV loaded successfully");
            mCameraView.enableView();
            mBgr = new Mat();
            break;
          default:
            super.onManagerConnected(status);
            break;
          }
        }
      }
    };
```

The concept of states (varying modes of operation) is central to Android activities
and `CameraActivity` is no exception. When the user selects a menu action to switch
the camera or take a photo, the effects are not just instantaneous. Actions affect
the work that must be done in subsequent frames. Some of this work is even done
asynchronously. Thus, many member variables of `CameraActivity` are dedicated
to tracking the logical state of the activity.

Understanding asynchronous event collisions in Android

Many Android library methods such as `startActivity()` do their
work asynchronously. While the work is being carried out, the user
may continue to use the interface, potentially initiating other work
that is logically inconsistent with the first work.

For example, suppose that `startActivity()` is called when a
certain button is clicked. If the user presses the button multiple times,
quickly, then more than one new activity may be pushed onto the
activity stack. This behavior is probably not what the developer or
user intended. A solution would be to disable the clicked button until
its activity resumes. Similar considerations affect our menu system in
`CameraActivity`.

Like any Android activity, `CameraActivity` also implements several callbacks that are executed in response to standard state changes, namely, changes in the activity lifecycle. Let's start by looking at the `onCreate()` and `onSaveInstanceState()` callbacks. These methods, respectively, are called at the beginning and end of the activity lifecycle. The `onCreate()` callback typically sets up the activity's view hierarchy, initializes data, and reads any saved data that may have been written last time `onSaveInstanceState()` was called.

> For details about the Android activity lifecycle, see
> the official documentation at `http://developer.`
> `android.com/reference/android/app/Activity.`
> `html#ActivityLifecycle`.

In `CameraActivity`, the `onCreate()` callback sets up the camera view and initializes data about the cameras. It also reads any previous data about the active camera that has been written by `onSaveInstanceState()`. Here are the implementations of the two methods:

```java
@SuppressLint("NewApi")
@Override
protected void onCreate(final Bundle savedInstanceState) {
  super.onCreate(savedInstanceState);

  final Window window = getWindow();
  window.addFlags(
    WindowManager.LayoutParams.FLAG_KEEP_SCREEN_ON);

  if (savedInstanceState != null) {
    mCameraIndex = savedInstanceState.getInt(
      STATE_CAMERA_INDEX, 0);
  } else {
    mCameraIndex = 0;
  }

  if (Build.VERSION.SDK_INT >=
    Build.VERSION_CODES.GINGERBREAD) {
    CameraInfo cameraInfo = new CameraInfo();
    Camera.getCameraInfo(mCameraIndex, cameraInfo);
    mIsCameraFrontFacing =
      (cameraInfo.facing ==
        CameraInfo.CAMERA_FACING_FRONT);
```

```
        mNumCameras = Camera.getNumberOfCameras();
    } else { // pre-Gingerbread
        // Assume there is only 1 camera and it is rear-facing.
        mIsCameraFrontFacing = false;
        mNumCameras = 1;
    }

    mCameraView = new NativeCameraView(this, mCameraIndex);
    mCameraView.setCvCameraViewListener(this);
    setContentView(mCameraView);
}

public void onSaveInstanceState(Bundle savedInstanceState) {
    // Save the current camera index.
    savedInstanceState.putInt(STATE_CAMERA_INDEX, mCameraIndex);

    super.onSaveInstanceState(savedInstanceState);
}
```

Note that certain data about the device's cameras are unavailable on Froyo (the oldest Android version that we support). To avoid runtime errors, we check `Build.VERSION.SDK_INT` before using the new APIs. Also, to avoid seeing unnecessary warnings in Eclipse, we add the `@SuppressLint("NewApi")` annotation to the declaration of `onCreate()`.

Several other activity lifecycle callbacks are also relevant to OpenCV. When the activity goes into the background (the `onPause()` callback) or finishes (the `onDestroy()` callback), the camera view should be disabled. When the activity comes into the foreground (the `onResume()` callback), the OpenCVLoader should attempt to initialize the library. (Remember that the camera view is enabled once the library is successfully initialized.) Here are the implementations of the relevant callbacks:

```
@Override
public void onPause() {
    if (mCameraView != null) {
        mCameraView.disableView();
    }
    super.onPause();
}
```

```
@Override
public void onResume() {
  super.onResume();
  OpenCVLoader.initAsync(OpenCVLoader.OPENCV_VERSION_2_4_3,
    this, mLoaderCallback);
  mIsMenuLocked = false;
}

@Override
public void onDestroy() {
  super.onDestroy();
  if (mCameraView != null) {
    mCameraView.disableView();
  }
}
```

Note that, in `onResume()`, we re-enable menu interaction. We do this in case it was previously disabled while pushing a child activity onto the stack.

At this point, our activity has the necessary code to set up a camera view and get data about the device's cameras. Next, we should implement the menu actions that enable the user to switch the camera and request that a photo be taken. Again, there are relevant activity lifecycle callbacks such as `onCreateOptionsMenu()` and `onOptionsItemSelected()`. In `onCreateOptionsMenu()`, we load our menu from its resource file. Then, if the device has only one camera, we remove the **Next Cam** menu item. In `onOptionsItemSelected()`, we handle the **Next Cam** menu item by cycling to the next camera index and then recreating the activity. (Remember that the camera index is saved in `onSaveInstanceState()` and restored in `onCreate()`, where it is used to construct the camera view.) We handle the **Take Photo** menu item by setting a Boolean value, which we check in an OpenCV callback later. In either case, we block any further handling of menu options until the current handling is complete (for example, until `onResume()`). Here is the implementation of the two menu-related callbacks:

```
@Override
  public boolean onCreateOptionsMenu(final Menu menu) {
    getMenuInflater().inflate(R.menu.activity_camera, menu);
    if (mNumCameras < 2) {
      // Remove the option to switch cameras, since there is
      // only 1.
      menu.removeItem(R.id.menu_next_camera);
    }
```

```
      return true;
    }


    @Override
    public boolean onOptionsItemSelected(final MenuItem item) {
      if (mIsMenuLocked) {
        return true;
      }
      switch (item.getItemId()) {
      case R.id.menu_next_camera:
        mIsMenuLocked = true;

        // With another camera index, recreate the activity.
        mCameraIndex++;
        if (mCameraIndex == mNumCameras) {
          mCameraIndex = 0;
        }
        recreate();

        return true;
      case R.id.menu_take_photo:
        mIsMenuLocked = true;

        // Next frame, take the photo.
        mIsPhotoPending = true;

        return true;
      default:
        return super.onOptionsItemSelected(item);
      }
    }
  }
```

Next, let's look at the callbacks that are required by the CvCameraViewListener2 interface. CameraActivity does not need to do anything when the camera feed starts (the onCameraViewStarted() callback) or stops (the onCameraViewStopped() callback), but it may need to perform some operations whenever a new frame arrives (the onCameraFrame() callback). First, if the user has requested a photo, one should be taken. (The photo capture functionality is actually quite complex, so we put it in a helper method, takePhoto(), which we will examine later in this section.)

Second, if the active camera is front-facing (that is, user-facing), the camera view should be mirrored (horizontally flipped), since people are accustomed to looking at themselves in a mirror, rather than from a camera's true perspective. OpenCV's `Core.flip()` method can be used to mirror the image. The arguments to, `Core. flip()` are a source `Mat`, a destination `Mat` (which may be the same as the source), and an integer indicating whether the flip should be vertical (0), horizontal (1), or both (-1). Here is the implementation of the `CvCameraViewListener2` callbacks:

```
@Override
public void onCameraViewStarted(final int width,
  final int height) {
}

@Override
public void onCameraViewStopped() {
}

@Override
public Mat onCameraFrame(final CvCameraViewFrame inputFrame) {
  final Mat rgba = inputFrame.rgba();

  if (mIsPhotoPending) {
    mIsPhotoPending = false;
      takePhoto(rgba);
  }

  if (mIsCameraFrontFacing) {
    // Mirror (horizontally flip) the preview.
    Core.flip(rgba, rgba, 1);
  }

  return rgba;
}
```

Now, finally, we are arriving at the function that will capture users' hearts and minds, or at least, their photos. As an argument, `takePhoto()` receives an RGBA color `Mat` that was read from the camera. We want to write this image to a disk, using an OpenCV method called `Highgui.imwrite()`. This method requires an image in BGR or BGRA color format, so first we must convert the RGBA image, using the `Improc.cvtColor()` method. Besides saving the image to a disk, we also want to enable other apps to find it via Android's `MediaStore`. To do so, we generate some metadata about the photo and then, using a `ContentResolver` object, we insert this metadata into `MediaStore` and get back a URI.

If we encounter a failure to save or insert the photo or insert it, we give up and call a helper method, onTakePhotoFailed(), which unlocks menu interaction and shows an error message to the user. On the other hand, if everything succeeds, we start LabActivity and pass it the data it needs to locate the saved photo. Here is the implementation of takePhoto() and onTakePhotoFailed():

```
private void takePhoto(final Mat rgba) {

    // Determine the path and metadata for the photo.
    final long currentTimeMillis = System.currentTimeMillis();
    final String appName = getString(R.string.app_name);
    final String galleryPath =
      Environment.getExternalStoragePublicDirectory(
        Environment.DIRECTORY_PICTURES).toString();
    final String albumPath = galleryPath + "/" + appName;
    final String photoPath = albumPath + "/" +
      currentTimeMillis + ".png";
    final ContentValues values = new ContentValues();
    values.put(MediaStore.MediaColumns.DATA, photoPath);
    values.put(Images.Media.MIME_TYPE,
      LabActivity.PHOTO_MIME_TYPE);
    values.put(Images.Media.TITLE, appName);
    values.put(Images.Media.DESCRIPTION, appName);
    values.put(Images.Media.DATE_TAKEN, currentTimeMillis);

    // Ensure that the album directory exists.
    File album = new File(albumPath);
    if (!album.isDirectory() && !album.mkdirs()) {
      Log.e(TAG, "Failed to create album directory at " +
        albumPath);
      onTakePhotoFailed();
      return;
    }

    // Try to create the photo.
    Imgproc.cvtColor(rgba, mBgr, Imgproc.COLOR_RGBA2BGR, 3);
    if (!Highgui.imwrite(photoPath, mBgr)) {
      Log.e(TAG, "Failed to save photo to " + photoPath);
      onTakePhotoFailed();
    }
    Log.d(TAG, "Photo saved successfully to " + photoPath);

    // Try to insert the photo into the MediaStore.
    Uri uri;
```

```java
      try {
        uri = getContentResolver().insert(
          Images.Media.EXTERNAL_CONTENT_URI, values);
      } catch (final Exception e) {
        Log.e(TAG, "Failed to insert photo into MediaStore");
        e.printStackTrace();

        // Since the insertion failed, delete the photo.
        File photo = new File(photoPath);
        if (!photo.delete()) {
          Log.e(TAG, "Failed to delete non-inserted photo");
        }

        onTakePhotoFailed();
        return;
      }

      // Open the photo in LabActivity.
      final Intent intent = new Intent(this, LabActivity.class);
      intent.putExtra(LabActivity.EXTRA_PHOTO_URI, uri);
      intent.putExtra(LabActivity.EXTRA_PHOTO_DATA_PATH,
        photoPath);
      startActivity(intent);
    }

    private void onTakePhotoFailed() {
      mIsMenuLocked = false;

      // Show an error message.
      final String errorMessage =
          getString(R.string.photo_error_message);
      runOnUiThread(new Runnable() {
        @Override
        public void run() {
          Toast.makeText(CameraActivity.this, errorMessage,
            Toast.LENGTH_SHORT).show();
        }
      });
    }
  }
```

For now, that's everything we want `CameraActivity` to do. We will expand this class in the following chapters, by adding more menu actions and handling them in the `onCameraFrame()` callback.

Deleting, editing, and sharing photos in LabActivity

Our second activity, LabActivity, needs to do the following:

- From the previous activity, receive a URI and file path for a PNG file
- Display the image that is contained in the PNG file
- Provide the following menu actions:
    - Show a confirmation dialog. On confirmation, delete the PNG file and finish the activity.
    - Show an intent chooser so that the user may select an app to edit the PNG file. (The URI is passed with the EDIT intent.)
    - Show a chooser so that the user may select an app to share or send the PNG file. (The URI is passed with the SEND intent.)

All of this functionality relies on standard Android library classes, notably the Intent class. **Intents** are the means by which activities communicate with each other. An activity receives an intent from its parent (the activity that created it) and may receive intents from its children (activities it created) as they finish. The communicating activities may be in different applications. An intent may contain key-value pairs called **extras**.

 For details about intents, see the official documentation at http://developer.android.com/guide/components/intents-filters.html.

LabActivity declares several public constants that are used by it and CameraActivity. These constants relate to images' metadata and to the extra keys that are used when CameraActivity and LabActivity communicate via intents. LabActivity also has member variables that are used to store the URI and path values, extracted from the extras. The onCreate() method does the work of extracting these values and setting up an image view that shows the PNG file. The implementation is as follows:

```
public class LabActivity extends Activity {

  public static final String PHOTO_MIME_TYPE = "image/png";

  public static final String EXTRA_PHOTO_URI =
    "com.nummist.secondsight.LabActivity.extra.PHOTO_URI";
  public static final String EXTRA_PHOTO_DATA_PATH =
    "com.nummist.secondsight.LabActivity.extra.PHOTO_DATA_PATH";
```

```
private Uri mUri;
private String mDataPath;

@Override
protected void onCreate(final Bundle savedInstanceState) {
  super.onCreate(savedInstanceState);

  final Intent intent = getIntent();
  mUri = intent.getParcelableExtra(EXTRA_PHOTO_URI);
  mDataPath = intent.getStringExtra(EXTRA_PHOTO_DATA_PATH);

  final ImageView imageView = new ImageView(this);
  imageView.setImageURI(mUri);

  setContentView(imageView);
}
```

The menu logic is simpler in LabActivity than in CameraActivity. All the menu actions of LabActivity result in a dialog or chooser being shown, and since a dialog or chooser blocks the rest of the user interface, we do not have to worry about blocking conflicting input ourselves. We just load the menu's resource file in onCreateOptionsMenu() and call a helper method for each possible action in onOptionsItemSelected(). The implementation is as follows:

```
@Override
public boolean onCreateOptionsMenu(final Menu menu) {
  getMenuInflater().inflate(R.menu.activity_lab, menu);
  return true;
}

@Override
public boolean onOptionsItemSelected(final MenuItem item) {
  switch (item.getItemId()) {
  case R.id.menu_delete:
    deletePhoto();
    return true;
  case R.id.menu_edit:
    editPhoto();
    return true;
  case R.id.menu_share:
    sharePhoto();
     return true;
  default:
    return super.onOptionsItemSelected(item);
  }
}
```

Let's examine the menu actions' helper methods one-by-one, starting with
deletePhoto(). Most of this method's implementation is the boilerplate code to
set up a confirmation dialog. The dialog's confirmation button has an onClick()
callback that deletes the image from the MediaStore and finishes the activity.
The implementation of deletePhoto() is as follows:

```
/*
 * Show a confirmation dialog. On confirmation, the photo is
 * deleted and the activity finishes.
 */
private void deletePhoto() {
  final AlertDialog.Builder alert = new AlertDialog.Builder(
    LabActivity.this);
  alert.setTitle(R.string.photo_delete_prompt_title);
  alert.setMessage(R.string.photo_delete_prompt_message);
  alert.setCancelable(false);
  alert.setPositiveButton(R.string.delete,
    new DialogInterface.OnClickListener() {
      @Override
        public void onClick(final DialogInterface dialog,
          final int which) {
          getContentResolver().delete(
            Images.Media.EXTERNAL_CONTENT_URI,
              MediaStore.MediaColumns.DATA + "=?",
                new String[] { mDataPath });
          finish();
        }
    });
  alert.setNegativeButton(android.R.string.cancel, null);
  alert.show();
}
```

The next helper method, editPhoto(), sets up an intent and starts a chooser for
that intent, using the Intent.createChooser() method. The user may cancel this
chooser or use it to select an activity. If an activity is selected, editPhoto() starts it.
The implementation is as follows:

```
/*
 * Show a chooser so that the user may pick an app for editing
 * the photo.
 */
```

```
private void editPhoto() {
  final Intent intent = new Intent(Intent.ACTION_EDIT);
  intent.setDataAndType(mUri, PHOTO_MIME_TYPE);
  startActivity(Intent.createChooser(intent,
    getString(R.string.photo_edit_chooser_title)));
}
```

The last helper method, sharePhoto(), is similar to editPhoto(), though the intent is configured differently. The implementation is as follows:

```
/*
 * Show a chooser so that the user may pick an app for sending
 * the photo.
 */
private void sharePhoto() {
  final Intent intent = new Intent(Intent.ACTION_SEND);
  intent.setType(PHOTO_MIME_TYPE);
  intent.putExtra(Intent.EXTRA_STREAM, mUri);
  intent.putExtra(Intent.EXTRA_SUBJECT,
    getString(R.string.photo_send_extra_subject));
  intent.putExtra(Intent.EXTRA_TEXT,
    getString(R.string.photo_send_extra_text));
  startActivity(Intent.createChooser(intent,
    getString(R.string.photo_send_chooser_title)));
}
}
```

That's the last functionality we need for a basic photo capture and sharing application. Now, we should be able to build and run Second Sight.

Summary

We have used OpenCV to create and show a live camera feed, and to save still images from this feed. We have also seen how to integrate the camera feed's lifecycle into the Android activity lifecycle, and how to share saved images across the boundaries of activities and applications.

The next chapter will expand our Second Sight app by adding various image filtering options to the menus of CameraActivity and LabActivity.

3
Applying Image Effects

For this chapter, our goal is to add several image filters to `Second Sight`. These filters rely on various OpenCV functions for manipulating matrices through splitting, merging, arithmetic operations, or applying lookup tables for complex functions. Certain filters also rely on a mathematics library called `Apache Commons Math`.

 The completed Eclipse project for this chapter can be downloaded from my website at `http://nummist.com/opencv/5206_03.zip`.

Adding files to the project

We need to add several files to our Eclipse project in order to create new types (that is, interfaces and classes) and to link to a new library, `Apache Commons Math`. The following are the new types that we want to create:

- `com.nummist.secondsight.filters.Filter`: It is an interface representing a filter that can be applied to an image.

- `com.nummist.secondsight.filters.NoneFilter`: It is a class representing a filter that does nothing. It implements the `Filter` interface.

- `com.nummist.secondsight.filters.convolution.StrokeEdgesFilter`: It is a class representing a filter that draws heavy-black lines atop edge regions. It implements the `Filter` interface.

- `com.nummist.secondsight.filters.curve.CurveFilter`: It is a class representing a filter that may apply a separate curvilinear transformation to each color channel in an image. (It is like **Curves** in Photoshop or Gimp.) It implements the `Filter` interface.

- `com.nummist.secondsight.filters.curve.CrossProcessCurveFilter`: It is a subclass of `CurveFilter`. It emulates a photo film processing technique called cross-processing.

- `com.nummist.secondsight.filters.curve.PortraCurveFilter`: It is a subclass of `CurveFilter`. It emulates a brand of photo film called Kodak Portra.

- `com.nummist.secondsight.filters.curve.ProviaCurveFilter`: It is a subclass of `CurveFilter`. It emulates a brand of photo film called Fuji Provia.

- `com.nummist.secondsight.filters.curve.VelviaCurveFilter`: It is a subclass of `CurveFilter`. It emulates a brand of photo film called Fuji Velvia.

- `com.nummist.secondsight.filters.curve.RecolorCMVFilter`: It is a class representing a filter that linearly combines color channels, such that the image appears to be mixed from a limited palette of cyan, magenta, and white. (It is like a specialization of **Channel Mixer** in Photoshop or Gimp.) It implements the `Filter` interface.

- `com.nummist.secondsight.filters.curve.RecolorRCFilter`: It is a class representing a filter that linearly combines color channels, such that the image appears to be mixed from a limited palette of red and cyan. (It is like a specialization of **Channel Mixer** in Photoshop or Gimp.) It implements the `Filter` interface.

- `com.nummist.secondsight.filters.curve.RecolorRGVFilter`: It is a class representing a filter that linearly combines color channels, such that the image appears to be mixed from a limited palette of red, green, and white. (It is like a specialization of **Channel Mixer** in Photoshop or Gimp.) It implements the `Filter` interface.

Create the appropriate packages and Java files under the `src` directory in the **Package Explorer** pane. (Right-click on the `src` directory and then choose **New | Package**, **New | Interface**, or **New | Class** from the context menu.)

Now, let's get the `Apache Commons Math` library. Download the latest version from `http://commons.apache.org/proper/commons-math/download_math.cgi`. Unzip the download file. Inside the unzipped folder, find a file with a name such as `commons-math3-3.2.jar`. (The version numbers may differ.) Copy this file into the `libs` folder of the Eclipse project.

After all the necessary files are added, your **Package Explorer** pane should look similar to the one in the following screenshot:

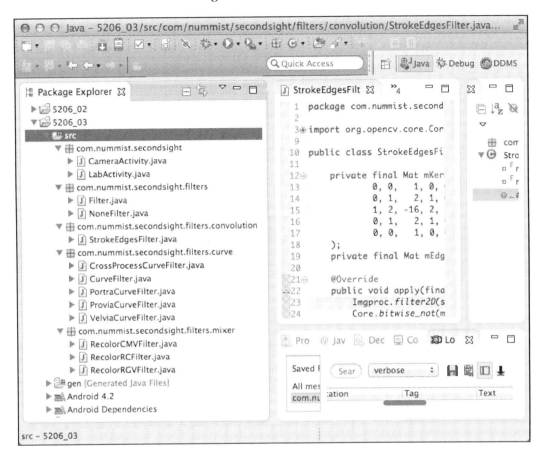

Defining the Filter interface

For our purposes, a filter is any transformation that can be applied to a source image and destination image. (The source and destination may be the same image or different images.) Our application needs to treat the filters interchangeably, so it is a good idea to formalize this definition of a filter's interface. Let's edit `Filter.java` so that the `Filter` interface is defined as follows:

```java
public interface Filter {
    public abstract void apply(final Mat src, final Mat dst);
}
```

As far as our app is concerned, the `apply` method is the only thing that our filters must have in common. Everything else is the implementation details.

The most basic implementation of the `Filter` interface is the `NoneFilter` class. As the name suggests, `NoneFilter` does no filtering at all. Let's implement it as follows:

```
public class NoneFilter implements Filter {
  @Override
  public void apply(final Mat src, final Mat dst) {
    // Do nothing.
  }
}
```

`NoneFilter` is just a convenient stand-in for other filters. We use it when we want to turn off filtering but still have an object that conforms to the `Filter` interface.

Mixing color channels

As we saw in *Chapter 2, Working with Camera Frames*, OpenCV stores image data in a matrix of type `Mat`, which is like a two-dimensional array. The columns and rows (specified by the first and second indices, respectively) correspond to the y and x pixel coordinates in the image. The elements are the pixel values. A pixel value may be represented by one number (in the case of a grayscale image) or multiple numbers (in the case of a color image). Each of these numbers is said to belong to a channel. A grayscale image may have just one channel, value (brightness), which is abbreviated as V. A color image may have as many as four channels—for example, red, green, blue, and alpha (transparency), which constitute the **RGBA** format. Other useful formats for color images include **RGB** (red, green, blue), **HSV** (hue, saturation, value), and **L*a*b** (luminosity, green-versus-magenta, yellow-versus-blue). In this book, we focus on RGB and RGBA images, but OpenCV supports other formats too. As we saw in the previous chapter, we can convert between color formats with the `Imgproc.cvtColor` static method.

If we separated the channels of an RGB image matrix, we could make three different grayscale image matrices, each having one channel. We could then apply some matrix arithmetic to these single-channel matrices, and merge the results to get another RGB image matrix. The resulting RGB image would look as if it were mixed from a different color palette than the original image was. This technique is called **channel mixing**. For an RGB image, we may define channel mixing in pseudocode as follows:

```
dst.b = funcB(src.b, src.g, src.r)
dst.g = funcG(src.b, src.g, src.r)
dst.r = funcR(src.b, src.g, src.r)
```

That is to say, each channel in the destination image is mapped from a function of any or all channels in the source image. We will not restrict our definition to any particular kind of function. However, let's note the visual effects of the following operations, which I find useful when working with RGB images:

- An average or weighted average appears to tint the output channel. For example, in pseudocode, if `dst.b = 0.5 * src.r + 0.5 * src.b`, image regions that were originally bluish become reddish or purplish.

- A `min` operation appears to desaturate the output channel. For example, in pseudocode, if `dst.b = min(src.r, src.g, src.b)`, blues become gray.

- A `max` operation appears to desaturate the output channel's complementary color. For example, in pseudocode, if `dst.b = max(src.r, src.g, src.b)`, yellows become gray. (Yellow is blue's complement, that is white minus blue is yellow, when we are dealing with the RGB color.)

With these effects in mind, let's look at the OpenCV functionality that we would use to produce them. OpenCV's `Core` class provides all the relevant functionality as static methods. The `Core.split(Mat m, List<Mat> mv)` method is responsible for channel splitting. As arguments, it takes a source matrix and a list of destination matrices. Each channel from the source is copied into a single-channel matrix in the destination list. If necessary, the destination list is populated with new matrices.

After using the `Core.split` method, we can apply matrix operations to the individual channels. The `Core.addWeighted(Mat src1, double alpha, Mat src2, double beta, double gamma, Mat dst)` method can be used to take a weighted average of two channels. The first four arguments are weights and source matrices. The fifth argument is a constant that is added to the result. The last argument is the destination matrix. In pseudocode, `dst = alpha * src1 + beta * src2 + gamma`.

> Generally, with methods in OpenCV, it is safe to pass a destination matrix that is also a source matrix. Of course, in this case, the values in the source matrix are overwritten. This is called an in-place operation.

The `Core.min(Mat src1, Mat src2, Mat dst)` and `Core.max(Mat src1, Mat src2, Mat dst)` methods each take a pair of source matrices and a destination matrix. These methods perform a per-element min or max.

Finally, the converse of `Core.split` is `Core.merge(List<Mat> mv, Mat m)`. We can use it to recreate a multichannel image from the split channels.

To do a practical example of channel mixing, let's open `RecolorRCFilter.java` and write the following implementation of the class:

```java
public class RecolorRCFilter implements Filter {
    private final ArrayList<Mat> mChannels = new ArrayList<Mat>(4);
    @Override
    public void apply(final Mat src, final Mat dst) {
        Core.split(src, mChannels);
        final Mat g = mChannels.get(1);
        final Mat b = mChannels.get(2);
        // dst.g = 0.5 * src.g + 0.5 * src.b
        Core.addWeighted(g, 0.5, b,  0.5, 0.0, g);
        // dst.b = dst.g
        mChannels.set(2, g);
        Core.merge(mChannels, dst);
    }
}
```

The effect of this filter is to turn greens and blues to cyan, leaving a limited color palette of red and cyan. It resembles the color palette of certain old movies and old computer games.

As a member variable, RecolorRCFilter has a list of four matrices. Whenever the apply() method is called, this list is populated with the four channels of the source matrix. (We assume that the source and destination matrices each have four channels, in RGBA order.) We get the green and blue channels (at indices 1 and 2 in the list), take their average, and assign the result back to the same channels. Last, we merge the four channels into the destination matrix, which may be the same as the source matrix.

The code for our other two channel mixing filters is similar, so, for brevity, we will omit most of it. Just note that RecolorRGVFilter relies on the following operations:

```
// dst.b = min(dst.r, dst.g, dst.b)
Core.min(b, r, b);
Core.min(b, g, b);
```

The effect of this filter is to desaturate blues, leaving a limited color palette of red, green, and white. It, too, resembles the color palette of certain old movies and old computer games.

Similarly, RecolorCMVFilter relies on the following operations:

```
// dst.b = max(dst.r, dst.g, dst.b)
Core.max(b, r, b);
Core.max(b, g, b);
```

The effect of this filter is to desaturate yellows, leaving a limited color palette of cyan, magenta, and white. Nobody ever made a movie in this color palette (yet!), but it will be a familiar sight to gamers of the 1980s.

Arbitrary channel mixing functions, in RGB, tend to produce effects that are bold and stylized, not subtle. This is true of our examples here. Next, let's look at a family of filters that are easier to parameterize for subtle, natural-looking results.

Making subtle color shifts with curves

When looking at a scene, we may pick up subtle cues from the way colors shift between different image regions. For example, outdoors on a clear day, shadows have a slightly blue tint due to the ambient light reflected from the blue sky, while highlights have a slightly yellow tint because they are in direct sunlight. When we see bluish shadows and yellowish highlights in a photograph, we may get a "warm and sunny" feeling. This effect may be natural, or it may be exaggerated by a filter.

Curve filters are useful for this type of manipulation. A curve filter is parameterized by sets of control points. For example, there might be one set of control points for each color channel. Each control point is a pair of numbers representing the input and output values for the given channel. For example, the pair (128, 180) means that a value of 128 in the given color channel is brightened to become a value of 180. Values between the control points are interpolated along a curve (hence the name, curve filter). In Gimp, a curve with the control points (0, 0), (128, 180), and (255, 255) is visualized as shown in the following screenshot:

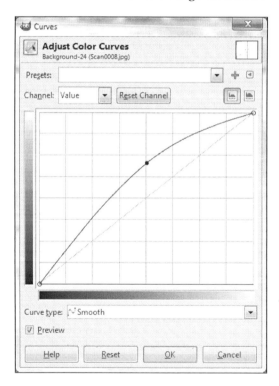

The x axis shows the input values ranging from 0 to 255, while the y axis shows the output values over the same range. Besides showing the curve, the graph shows the line y = x (no change) for comparison.

Curvilinear interpolation helps to ensure that color transitions are smooth, not abrupt. Thus, a curve filter makes it relatively easy to create subtle, natural-looking effects. We may define an RGB curve filter in pseudocode as follows:

```
dst.b = funcB(src.b) where funcB interpolates pointsB
dst.g = funcG(src.g) where funcG interpolates pointsG
dst.r = funcR(src.r) where funcR interpolates pointsR
```

For now, we will work with RGB and RGBA curve filters, and with channel values that range from 0 to 255. If we want such a curve filter to produce natural-looking results, we should use the following rules of thumb:

- Every set of control points should include (0, 0) and (255, 255). This way, black remains black, white remains white, and the image does not appear to have an overall tint.

- As the input value increases, the output value should always increase too. (Their relationship should be monotonically increasing.) This way, shadows remain shadows, highlights remain highlights, and the image does not appear to have inconsistent lighting or contrast.

OpenCV does not provide curvilinear interpolation functions but the Apache Commons Math library does. (See *Adding files to the project*, earlier in this chapter, for instructions on setting up Apache Commons Math.) This library provides interfaces called UnivariateInterpolator and UnivariateFunction, which have implementations including LinearInterpolator, SplineInterpolator, LinearFunction, and PolynomialSplineFunction. (Splines are a type of curve.) UnivariateInterpolator has an instance method, interpolate(double[] xval, double[] yval), which takes arrays of input and output values for the control points and returns a UnivariateFunction object. The UnivariateFunction object can provide interpolated values via the method value(double x).

 API documentation for Apache Commons Math is available at http://commons.apache.org/proper/commons-math/apidocs/.

These interpolation functions are computationally expensive. We do not want to run them again and again for every channel of every pixel and every frame. Fortunately, we do not have to. There are only 256 possible input values per channel, so it is practical to precompute all possible output values and store them in a lookup table. For OpenCV's purposes, a lookup table is a Mat object whose indices represent input values and whose elements represent output values. The lookup can be performed using the static method Core.LUT(Mat src, Mat lut, Mat dst). In pseudocode, dst = lut[src]. The number of elements in lut should match the range of values in src, and the number of channels in lut should match the number of channels in src.

Now, using Apache Commons Math and OpenCV, let's implement a curve filter for RGBA images with channel values ranging from 0 to 255. Open CurveFilter.java and write the following code:

```
public class CurveFilter implements Filter {
  // The lookup table.
  private final Mat mLUT = new MatOfInt();
  public CurveFilter(
    final double[] vValIn, final double[] vValOut,
    final double[] rValIn, final double[] rValOut,
    final double[] gValIn, final double[] gValOut,
    final double[] bValIn, final double[] bValOut) {
    // Create the interpolation functions.
    UnivariateFunction vFunc = newFunc(vValIn, vValOut);
    UnivariateFunction rFunc = newFunc(rValIn, rValOut);
    UnivariateFunction gFunc = newFunc(gValIn, gValOut);
    UnivariateFunction bFunc = newFunc(bValIn, bValOut);
    // Create and populate the lookup table.
    mLUT.create(256, 1, CvType.CV_8UC4);
    for (int i = 0; i < 256; i++) {
      final double v = vFunc.value(i);
      final double r = rFunc.value(v);
      final double g = gFunc.value(v);
      final double b = bFunc.value(v);
      mLUT.put(i, 0, r, g, b, i); // alpha is unchanged
    }
  }
  @Override
  public void apply(final Mat src, final Mat dst) {
    // Apply the lookup table.
    Core.LUT(src, mLUT, dst);
  }
  private UnivariateFunction newFunc(final double[] valIn,
    final double[] valOut) {
    UnivariateInterpolator interpolator;
    if (valIn.length > 2) {
      interpolator = new SplineInterpolator();
    } else {
      interpolator = new LinearInterpolator();
    }
    return interpolator.interpolate(valIn, valOut);
  }
}
```

`CurveFilter` stores the lookup table in a member variable. The constructor method populates the lookup table based on the four sets of control points that are taken as arguments. As well as a set of control points for each of the RGB channels, the constructor also takes a set of control points for the image's overall brightness, just for convenience. A helper method, `newFunc`, creates an appropriate interpolation function (linear or spline) for each set of control points. Then, we iterate over the possible input values and populate the lookup table.

The `apply` method is a one-liner. It simply uses the precomputed lookup table with the given source and destination matrices.

CurveFilter can be subclassed to define a filter with a specific set of control points. For example, let's open `PortraCurveFilter.java` and write the following code:

```java
public class PortraCurveFilter extends CurveFilter {
  public PortraCurveFilter() {
    super(
      new double[] { 0, 23, 157, 255 }, // vValIn
      new double[] { 0, 20, 173, 255 }, // vValOut
      new double[] { 0, 69, 213, 255 }, // rValIn
      new double[] { 0, 69, 218, 255 }, // rValOut
      new double[] { 0, 52, 189, 255 }, // gValIn
      new double[] { 0, 47, 196, 255 }, // gValOut
      new double[] { 0, 41, 231, 255 }, // bValIn
      new double[] { 0, 46, 228, 255 }); // bValOut
  }
}
```

This filter brightens the image, makes shadows cooler (more blue), and makes highlights warmer (more yellow). It produces flattering skin tones and tends to make things look sunnier and cleaner. It resembles the color characteristics of a brand of photo film called Kodak Portra, which was often used for portraits.

The code for our other three channel mixing filters is similar. The `ProviaCurveFilter` class uses the following arguments for its control points:

```java
      new double[] { 0, 255 }, // vValIn
      new double[] { 0, 255 }, // vValOut
      new double[] { 0, 59, 202, 255 }, // rValIn
      new double[] { 0, 54, 210, 255 }, // rValOut
      new double[] { 0, 27, 196, 255 }, // gValIn
      new double[] { 0, 21, 207, 255 }, // gValOut
      new double[] { 0, 35, 205, 255 },  // bValIn
      new double[] { 0, 25, 227, 255 }); // bValOut
```

The effect of this filter is to increase the contrast between shadows and highlights, and make the image slightly cool (bluish) throughout most tones. Sky, water, and shade are accentuated more than sun. It resembles a brand of photo film called Fuji Provia, which was often used for landscapes.

The `VelviaCurveFilter` class uses the following arguments for its control points:

```
new double[] { 0, 128, 221, 255 }, // vValIn
new double[] { 0, 118, 215, 255 }, // vValOut
new double[] { 0, 25, 122, 165, 255 }, // rValIn
new double[] { 0, 21, 153, 206, 255 }, // rValOut
new double[] { 0, 25,  95, 181, 255 }, // gValIn
new double[] { 0, 21, 102, 208, 255 }, // gValOut
new double[] { 0, 35, 205, 255 },  // bValIn
new double[] { 0, 25, 227, 255 }); // bValOut
```

The effect of this filter is to produce deep shadows and vivid colors. It resembles a brand of photo film called Fuji Velvia, which was often used to produce landscapes, with azure skies in daytime or crimson clouds at sunset.

Finally, the `CrossProcessCurveFilter` class uses the following arguments for its control points:

```
new double[] { 0, 255 }, // vValIn
new double[] { 0, 255 }, // vValOut
new double[] { 0, 56, 211, 255 }, // rValIn
new double[] { 0, 22, 255, 255 }, // rValOut
new double[] { 0, 56, 208, 255 }, // gValIn
new double[] { 0, 39, 226, 255 }, // gValOut
new double[] {  0, 255 },  // bValIn
new double[] { 20, 235 }); // bValOut
```

The effect is a strong, blue or greenish-blue tint in shadows and a strong, yellow or greenish-yellow tint in highlights. It resembles a film processing technique called cross-processing, which was sometimes used to produce grungy-looking photos of fashion models, pop stars, and so on.

For a good discussion of how to emulate various brands of photo film, see Petteri Sulonen's blog at `http://www.prime-junta.net/pont/How_to/100_Curves_and_Films/_Curves_and_films.html`. The control points that we use are based on examples given in this article.

Curve filters are a convenient tool for manipulating color and contrast, but they are limited insofar as each destination pixel is affected by only a single input pixel. Next, we will examine a more flexible family of filters, which enable each destination pixel to be affected by a neighborhood of input pixels.

Processing a neighborhood of pixels with convolution filters

For a convolution filter, the channel values at each output pixel are a weighted average of the corresponding channel values in a neighborhood of input pixels. We can put the weights in a matrix, called a **convolution matrix** or **kernel**. For example, consider the following kernel:

```
{{ 0, -1,  0},
 {-1,  4, -1},
 { 0, -1,  0}}
```

The central element is the weight for the source pixel that has the same indices as of the destination pixel. Other elements represent weights for the rest of the neighborhood of input pixels. Here, we are considering a 3 x 3 neighborhood. However, OpenCV supports kernels with any square and odd-numbered dimensions. This particular kernel is a type of edge-finding filter called a **Laplacian** filter. For a neighborhood of flat (same) color, it yields a black output pixel. For a neighborhood of high contrast, it yields a bright output pixel.

Let's consider another kernel where the central element is greater by 1:

```
{{ 0, -1,  0},
 {-1,  5, -1},
 { 0, -1,  0}}
```

This is equivalent to taking the result of a Laplacian filter and then adding it to the original image. Instead of edge-finding, we get edge-sharpening. That is, edge regions get brighter while the rest of the image remains unchanged.

> **Beware big kernels**
>
> The bigger the kernel, the more expensive the computation. Kernels larger than 5 x 5 (that is, 25 input pixels per output pixel) are probably not practical for live video processing on typical Android devices today.

OpenCV provides many static methods for convolution filters that use certain popular kernels. The following are some examples:

- `Imgproc.blur(Mat src, Mat dst, Size ksize)`: It blurs the image by taking a simple average of a neighborhood of size `ksize`. For example, if `ksize` is `new Size(5, 5)`, then the kernel is the following:

  ```
  {{0.04, 0.04, 0.04, 0.04, 0.04},
   {0.04, 0.04, 0.04, 0.04, 0.04},
   {0.04, 0.04, 0.04, 0.04, 0.04},
   {0.04, 0.04, 0.04, 0.04, 0.04},
   {0.04, 0.04, 0.04, 0.04, 0.04}}
  ```

- `Laplacian(Mat src, Mat dst, int ddepth, int ksize, double scale, double delta)`: It is a Laplacian edge-finding filter, as described previously. Results are multiplied by a constant (the scale argument) and added to another constant (the delta argument).

Moreover, OpenCV provides a static method, `Imgproc.filter2D(Mat src, Mat dst, int ddepth, Mat kernel)`, which enables us to specify our own kernels. For learning purposes, we will take this approach. The `ddepth` argument determines the numeric type of the destination's data. This argument may be any of the following:

- `-1`: It means the same numeric type as in the source.
- `CvType.CV_16S`: It means 16-bit signed integers.
- `CvType.CV_32F`: It means 32-bit floats.
- `CvType.CV_64F`: It means 64-bit floats.

Let's use a convolution filter as part of a more complex filter that draws heavy, black lines atop edge regions in the image. To achieve this effect, we also rely on two more static methods from OpenCV:

- `Core.bitwise_not(Mat src, Mat dst)`: This method inverts the image's brightness and colors, such that white becomes black, red becomes cyan, and so on. It is useful to us because our convolution filter will produce white edges on a black field, whereas we want the opposite: black edges on a white field.

- `Core.multiply(Mat src1, Mat src2, Mat dst, double scale)`: This method blends a pair of images by multiplying their values together. The resulting values are scaled by a constant (the `scale` argument). For example, `scale` can be used to normalize the product to the [0, 255] range. For our purposes, `Core.multiply` can serve to superimpose the black edges on the original image.

The following is the implementation of the blackened edge effect in
`StrokeEdgesFilter`:

```
public class StrokeEdgesFilter implements Filter {
  private final Mat mKernel = new MatOfInt(
      0, 0,   1, 0, 0,
      0, 1,   2, 1, 0,
      1, 2, -16, 2, 1,
      0, 1,   2, 1, 0,
      0, 0,   1, 0, 0
  );
  private final Mat mEdges = new Mat();
  @Override
  public void apply(final Mat src, final Mat dst) {
    Imgproc.filter2D(src, mEdges, -1, mKernel);
    Core.bitwise_not(mEdges, mEdges);
    Core.multiply(src, mEdges, dst, 1.0/255.0);
  }
}
```

We will look at some other complex uses of convolution filters in subsequent
chapters.

Next, let's add a user interface for enabling and disabling all our filters.

Adding the filters to CameraActivity

We will let the user have up to one channel mixing filter, one curve filter, and one
convolution filter active at any time. For each filter category, we will provide a menu
button that lets the user cycle through the available filters, or no filter.

Let's start by editing the relevant resource files to define the menu buttons and their
text. We should add the following strings in `res/values/strings.xml`:

```
<string name="menu_next_curve_filter">Next Curve</string>
<string name="menu_next_mixer_filter">Next Mixer</string>
<string name="menu_next_convolution_filter">Next Kernel</string>
```

Then, we should edit `res/menu/activity_camera.xml` as follows:

```
<menu xmlns:android="http://schemas.android.com/apk/res/android">
  <item
    android:id="@+id/menu_next_curve_filter"
    android:orderInCategory="100"
    android:showAsAction="ifRoom|withText"
    android:title="@string/menu_next_curve_filter" />
```

```xml
<item
  android:id="@+id/menu_next_mixer_filter"
  android:orderInCategory="100"
  android:showAsAction="ifRoom|withText"
  android:title="@string/menu_next_mixer_filter" />
<item
  android:id="@+id/menu_next_convolution_filter"
  android:orderInCategory="100"
  android:showAsAction="ifRoom|withText"
  android:title="@string/menu_next_convolution_filter" />
<item
  android:id="@+id/menu_next_camera"
  android:orderInCategory="100"
  android:showAsAction="ifRoom|withText"
  android:title="@string/menu_next_camera" />
<item
  android:id="@+id/menu_take_photo"
  android:orderInCategory="100"
  android:showAsAction="always|withText"
  android:title="@string/menu_take_photo" />
</menu>
```

To store the information about the available and selected filters, we need several new variables in `CameraActivity`. The available filters are just `Filter[]` arrays. The indices of the selected filters are stored in the same way as the index of the selected camera device, that is, by serializing and deserializing (saving and restoring) an integer to/from an Android `Bundle` object. The following are the variable declarations that we must add to `CameraActivity`:

```java
// Keys for storing the indices of the active filters.
private static final String STATE_CURVE_FILTER_INDEX =
  "curveFilterIndex";
private static final String STATE_MIXER_FILTER_INDEX =
  "mixerFilterIndex";
private static final String STATE_CONVOLUTION_FILTER_INDEX =
  "convolutionFilterIndex";
// The filters.
private Filter[] mCurveFilters;
private Filter[] mMixerFilters;
private Filter[] mConvolutionFilters;
// The indices of the active filters.
private int mCurveFilterIndex;
private int mMixerFilterIndex;
private int mConvolutionFilterIndex;
```

Since our `Filter` implementations rely on classes in OpenCV they cannot be instantiated until the OpenCV library is loaded. Thus, our `BaseLoaderCallback` object is responsible for initializing the `Filter[]` arrays. We should edit it as follows:

```
private BaseLoaderCallback mLoaderCallback =
  new BaseLoaderCallback(this) {
  @Override
  public void onManagerConnected(final int status) {
    switch (status) {
      case LoaderCallbackInterface.SUCCESS:
        Log.d(TAG, "OpenCV loaded successfully");
      mCameraView.enableView();
      mBgr = new Mat();
      mCurveFilters = new Filter[] {
        new NoneFilter(),
        new PortraCurveFilter(),
        new ProviaCurveFilter(),
        new VelviaCurveFilter(),
        new CrossProcessCurveFilter()
      };
      mMixerFilters = new Filter[] {
        new NoneFilter(),
        new RecolorRCFilter(),
        new RecolorRGVFilter(),
        new RecolorCMVFilter()
      };
      mConvolutionFilters = new Filter[] {
        new NoneFilter(),
        new StrokeEdgesFilter()
      };
      break;
      default:
      super.onManagerConnected(status);
      break;
    }
  }
};
```

The onCreate method can initialize the selected filter indices or load them from the savedInstanceState argument. Let's edit the method as follows:

```
protected void onCreate(final Bundle savedInstanceState) {
  super.onCreate(savedInstanceState);
  final Window window = getWindow();
  window.addFlags(
```

```
      WindowManager.LayoutParams.FLAG_KEEP_SCREEN_ON);
    if (savedInstanceState != null) {
      mCameraIndex = savedInstanceState.getInt(
        STATE_CAMERA_INDEX, 0);
      mCurveFilterIndex = savedInstanceState.getInt(
        STATE_CURVE_FILTER_INDEX, 0);
      mMixerFilterIndex = savedInstanceState.getInt(
        STATE_MIXER_FILTER_INDEX, 0);
      mConvolutionFilterIndex = savedInstanceState.getInt(
        STATE_CONVOLUTION_FILTER_INDEX, 0);
    } else {
      mCameraIndex = 0;
      mCurveFilterIndex = 0;
      mMixerFilterIndex = 0;
      mConvolutionFilterIndex = 0;
    }
  // ...
  }
```

Similarly, the onSaveInstanceState method should save the selected filter indices to the savedInstanceState argument. Let's edit the method as follows:

```
  public void onSaveInstanceState(Bundle savedInstanceState) {
    // Save the current camera index.
    savedInstanceState.putInt(STATE_CAMERA_INDEX, mCameraIndex);
    // Save the current filter indices.
    savedInstanceState.putInt(STATE_CURVE_FILTER_INDEX,
      mCurveFilterIndex);
    savedInstanceState.putInt(STATE_MIXER_FILTER_INDEX,
      mMixerFilterIndex);
    savedInstanceState.putInt(STATE_CONVOLUTION_FILTER_INDEX,
      mConvolutionFilterIndex);
    super.onSaveInstanceState(savedInstanceState);
  }
```

To make each of the new menu items functional, we just need to add some boilerplate code that updates the relevant filter index. Let's edit the onOptionsItemSelected method as follows:

```
  public boolean onOptionsItemSelected(final MenuItem item) {
    if (mIsMenuLocked) {
      return true;
    }
    switch (item.getItemId()) {
      case R.id.menu_next_curve_filter:
```

```
      mCurveFilterIndex++;
      if (mCurveFilterIndex == mCurveFilters.length) {
        mCurveFilterIndex = 0;
      }
      return true;
    case R.id.menu_next_mixer_filter:
      mMixerFilterIndex++;
      if (mMixerFilterIndex == mMixerFilters.length) {
        mMixerFilterIndex = 0;
      }
      return true;
    case R.id.menu_next_convolution_filter:
      mConvolutionFilterIndex++;
      if (mConvolutionFilterIndex ==
        mConvolutionFilters.length) {
        mConvolutionFilterIndex = 0;
      }
      return true;
    // ...
    default:
      return super.onOptionsItemSelected(item);
    }
  }
```

Now, in the onCameraFrame callback method, we should apply each selected filter to the image. The following is the new implementation:

```
public Mat onCameraFrame(final CvCameraViewFrame inputFrame) {
  final Mat rgba = inputFrame.rgba();
  // Apply the active filters.
  mCurveFilters[mCurveFilterIndex].apply(rgba, rgba);
  mMixerFilters[mMixerFilterIndex].apply(rgba, rgba);
  mConvolutionFilters[mConvolutionFilterIndex].apply(
    rgba, rgba);
  if (mIsPhotoPending) {
    mIsPhotoPending = false;
    takePhoto(rgba);
  }
  if (mIsCameraFrontFacing) {
    // Mirror (horizontally flip) the preview.
    Core.flip(rgba, rgba, 1);
  }
  return rgba;
}
```

That's all! Run the app, select filters, take some photos, and share them. As an example of how the app should look, here is a screenshot with `RecolorRCFilter` and `StrokeEdgesFilter` enabled:

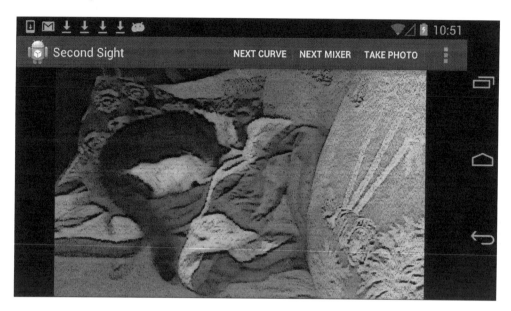

Summary

`Second Sight` now has some functionality that is more interesting than just reading and sharing camera data. Several filters can be selected and combined to give a stylized or vintage look to our photos. These filters are efficient enough to apply to live video too, so we use them in the preview mode as well as the saved photos.

Although photo filters are fun, they are only the most basic use of OpenCV. Before we can truly say we have made a computer vision application, we need to make the app respond differently depending on what it is seeing. This goal will be the focus of the next chapter.

4
Recognizing and Tracking Images

Our goal in this chapter is to add image tracking to Second Sight. We will train the app to recognize certain arbitrary, rectangular images—for example, paintings—and to determine their pose in a 2D projection. The app will draw an outline around a tracked image when it appears in the camera feed. All of the tracking and drawing is done using OpenCV rather than other Android libraries.

 The complete Eclipse project for this chapter can be downloaded from my website at http://nummist.com/opencv/5206_04.zip.

Adding files to the project

For this chapter, we need to add just one new class, com.nummist.secondsight. filters.ar.ImageDetectionFilter. We also need to add some resource files, that is, the images that we want to track. Download the images from http://nummist. com/opencv/5206_04_images.zip, unzip them, and put them in the project's res/ drawable-nodpi folder.

These images are famous paintings by a Dutch artist named Vincent van Gogh and an Indian artist named Basawan. Our tracker will work well with these images because they contain many high-contrast details, without much repetition of patterns. Thus, there is something distinctive to track in most of the parts of each image. For example, here is one of Basawan's paintings, *Akbar Hunting with Cheetahs*:

And here is one of Van Gogh's paintings, *The Starry Night*:

Understanding image tracking

Imagine the following conversation:

> *Person A: I can't find my print of The Starry Night. Do you know where it is?*

> *Person B: What does it look like?*

For a computer, or for someone who is naive about Western art, Person B's question is quite reasonable. Before we can use our sense of sight (or other senses) to track something, we need to have sensed that thing before. (Failing that, we at least need a good description of what we will sense.) For computer vision, we must provide a reference image that will be compared with the live camera image or scene. If the target has complex geometry or moving parts, we might need to provide many reference images to account for different perspectives and poses. However, for our examples using famous paintings, we will assume that the target is rectangular and rigid.

For this chapter's purposes, let's say that the goal of tracking is to determine how our rectangular target is posed in 3D. With this information, we can draw an outline around our target. In the final 2D image, the outline will be a quadrilateral (not necessarily a rectangle), since the target could be skewed away from the camera.

There are four major steps in this type of tracking:

1. Find **features** in the reference image and scene. A feature is a point that is likely to maintain a similar appearance when viewed from different distances or angles. For example, corners often have this characteristic.

2. Find **descriptors** for each set of features. A descriptor is a vector of data about a feature. Some features are not suitable for generating a descriptor, so an image has fewer descriptors than features.

3. Find **matches** between the two sets of descriptors. If we imagine the descriptors as points in a multidimensional space, a match is defined in terms of some measure of distance between points. Descriptors that are close enough to each other are considered a match.

4. Find the **homography** between a reference image and a matching image in the scene. A homography is a 3D transformation that would be necessary to line up the two projected 2D images (or come as close as possible to lining them up). It is calculated based on the two images' matching feature points. By applying the homography to a rectangle, we can get an outline of the tracked object.

There are many different techniques for performing each of the first three steps. OpenCV provides relevant classes called `FeatureDetector`, `DescriptorExtractor`, and `DescriptorMatcher`, each supporting several techniques. We will use a combination of techniques that OpenCV calls `FeatureDetector.STAR`, `DescriptorExtractor.FREAK`, and `DescriptorMatcher.BRUTEFORCE_HAMMING`. This combination is relatively fast and robust. Unlike some alternatives, it is **scale-invariant** and **rotation-invariant**, meaning that the target can be tracked from various distances and perspectives. Also, unlike some other alternatives, it is not patented so it is free for use even in commercial applications.

For a mathematical description of **FREAK** and its merits relative to other descriptor extractors, see the paper *FREAK: Fast Retina Keypoint* by Alahi, Ortiz, and Vandergheynst. An electronic version of the paper is available at `http://infoscience.epfl.ch/record/175537/files/2069.pdf`.

Writing an image tracking filter

We will write our tracker as an implementation of the `Filter` interface, which we created in the previous chapter. The tracker's class name will be `ImageDetectionFilter`. As member variables, this class has instances of `FeatureDetector`, `DescriptorExtractor`, and `DescriptorMatcher`, as well as several `Mat` instances that store image data and intermediate or final results of tracking calculations. Some of these results are stored because they do not change from frame to frame. Others are stored simply because it is more efficient than recreating the `Mat` instance for each frame. The declarations of the class and member variables are as follows:

```
public class ImageDetectionFilter implements Filter {

  private final Mat mReferenceImage;
  private final MatOfKeyPoint mReferenceKeypoints =
    new MatOfKeyPoint();
  private final Mat mReferenceDescriptors = new Mat();
  // CVType defines the color depth, number of channels, and
  // channel layout in the image.
  private final Mat mReferenceCorners =
    new Mat(4, 1, CvType.CV_32FC2);

  private final MatOfKeyPoint mSceneKeypoints =
    new MatOfKeyPoint();
  private final Mat mSceneDescriptors = new Mat();
  private final Mat mCandidateSceneCorners =
    new Mat(4, 1, CvType.CV_32FC2);
  private final Mat mSceneCorners = new Mat(4, 1,
    CvType.CV_32FC2);
  private final MatOfPoint mIntSceneCorners = new MatOfPoint();

  private final Mat mGraySrc = new Mat();
  private final MatOfDMatch mMatches = new MatOfDMatch();

  private final FeatureDetector mFeatureDetector =
    FeatureDetector.create(FeatureDetector.STAR);
  private final DescriptorExtractor mDescriptorExtractor =
    DescriptorExtractor.create(DescriptorExtractor.FREAK);
  private final DescriptorMatcher mDescriptorMatcher =
    DescriptorMatcher.create(
      DescriptorMatcher.BRUTEFORCE_HAMMING);

  private final Scalar mLineColor = new Scalar(0, 255, 0);
```

We want a convenient way to make an image tracker for any arbitrary image. We can package images with our app as so-called **drawable** resources, which can be loaded by any Android `Context` subclass such as `Activity`. Thus, we provide a constructor, `ImageDetectionFilter(final Context context, final int referenceImageResourceID)`, which loads the reference image with the given `Context` and resource identifier. RGBA and grayscale versions of the image are stored in the member variables. The image's corner points are also stored, and so are its features and descriptors. Its code is as follows:

```
public ImageDetectionFilter(final Context context,
    final int referenceImageResourceID) throws IOException {

  mReferenceImage = Utils.loadResource(context,
    referenceImageResourceID,
      Highgui.CV_LOAD_IMAGE_COLOR);

  final Mat referenceImageGray = new Mat();
  Imgproc.cvtColor(mReferenceImage, referenceImageGray,
    Imgproc.COLOR_BGR2GRAY);
  Imgproc.cvtColor(mReferenceImage, mReferenceImage,
    Imgproc.COLOR_BGR2RGBA);

  mReferenceCorners.put(0, 0,
    new double[] {0.0, 0.0});
  mReferenceCorners.put(1, 0,
    new double[] {referenceImageGray.cols(), 0.0});
  mReferenceCorners.put(2, 0,
    new double[] {referenceImageGray.cols(),
      referenceImageGray.rows()});
  mReferenceCorners.put(3, 0,
    new double[] {0.0, referenceImageGray.rows()});

  mFeatureDetector.detect(referenceImageGray,
    mReferenceKeypoints);
  mDescriptorExtractor.compute(referenceImageGray,
    mReferenceKeypoints, mReferenceDescriptors);
}
```

Recall that the `Filter` interface declares a method, `apply(final Mat src, final Mat dst)`. Our implementation of this method applies the feature detector, descriptor extractor, and descriptor matcher to a grayscale version of the source image. Then, we call helper functions that find the four corners of the tracked target (if any), and draw the quadrilateral outline. The code is as follows:

```
@Override
public void apply(final Mat src, final Mat dst) {
    Imgproc.cvtColor(src, mGraySrc, Imgproc.COLOR_RGBA2GRAY);

    mFeatureDetector.detect(mGraySrc, mSceneKeypoints);
    mDescriptorExtractor.compute(mGraySrc, mSceneKeypoints,
        mSceneDescriptors);
    mDescriptorMatcher.match(mSceneDescriptors,
        mReferenceDescriptors, mMatches);

    findSceneCorners();
    draw(src, dst);
}
```

The `findSceneCorners()` helper method is a bigger block of code, but a lot of it simply iterates through the matches to assemble a list of the best ones. If all the matches are really bad (as indicated by a large distance value), we assume that the target is not in the scene and we clear any previous estimate of its corner locations. If the matches are not really bad, but are not really good either, we assume that the target is somewhere in the scene but we keep our previous estimate of its corner locations. This policy helps to stabilize the estimate of the corner locations. Finally, if the matches are good and there are at least four of them, we find the homography and use it to update the estimated corner locations.

For a mathematical description of finding the homography, see the official OpenCV documentation at `http://docs.opencv.org/modules/calib3d/doc/camera_calibration_and_3d_reconstruction.html?highlight=findhomography#findhomography`.

The implementation of `findSceneCorners()` is as follows:

```
private void findSceneCorners() {

  List<DMatch> matchesList = mMatches.toList();
  if (matchesList.size() < 4) {
    // There are too few matches to find the homography.
    return;
  }

  List<KeyPoint> referenceKeypointsList =
    mReferenceKeypoints.toList();
  List<KeyPoint> sceneKeypointsList =
    mSceneKeypoints.toList();

  // Calculate the max and min distances between keypoints.
  double maxDist = 0.0;
  double minDist = Double.MAX_VALUE;
  for(DMatch match : matchesList) {
    double dist = match.distance;
    if (dist < minDist) {
      minDist = dist;
    }
    if (dist > maxDist) {
      maxDist = dist;
    }
  }

  // The thresholds for minDist are chosen subjectively
  // based on testing. The unit is not related to pixel
  // distances; it is related to the number of failed tests
  // for similarity between the matched descriptors.
  if (minDist > 50.0) {
    // The target is completely lost.
    // Discard any previously found corners.
    mSceneCorners.create(0, 0, mSceneCorners.type());
    return;
  } else if (minDist > 25.0) {
    // The target is lost but maybe it is still close.
    // Keep any previously found corners.
    return;
  }
```

```
// Identify "good" keypoints based on match distance.
ArrayList<Point> goodReferencePointsList =
  new ArrayList<Point>();
ArrayList<Point> goodScenePointsList =
  new ArrayList<Point>();
double maxGoodMatchDist = 1.75 * minDist;
for(DMatch match : matchesList) {
  if (match.distance < maxGoodMatchDist) {
    goodReferencePointsList.add(
      referenceKeypointsList.get(match.trainIdx).pt);
    goodScenePointsList.add(
      sceneKeypointsList.get(match.queryIdx).pt);
  }
}

if (goodReferencePointsList.size() < 4 ||
    goodScenePointsList.size() < 4) {
  // There are too few good points to find the homography.
  return;
}

MatOfPoint2f goodReferencePoints = new MatOfPoint2f();
goodReferencePoints.fromList(goodReferencePointsList);

MatOfPoint2f goodScenePoints = new MatOfPoint2f();
goodScenePoints.fromList(goodScenePointsList);

Mat homography = Calib3d.findHomography(
  goodReferencePoints, goodScenePoints);
Core.perspectiveTransform(mReferenceCorners,
  mCandidateSceneCorners, homography);

mCandidateSceneCorners.convertTo(mIntSceneCorners,
  CvType.CV_32S);
if (Imgproc.isContourConvex(mIntSceneCorners)) {
  mCandidateSceneCorners.copyTo(mSceneCorners);
}
}
```

Our other helper method, draw(Mat src, Mat dst), starts by copying the source image to the destination. Then, if the target is not being tracked, we draw a thumbnail of it in a corner of the image, so that the user knows what to seek. If the target is being tracked, we draw an outline around it. The code is as follows:

```
protected void draw(Mat src, Mat dst) {

  if (dst != src) {
    src.copyTo(dst);
  }

  if (mSceneCorners.height() < 4) {
    // The target has not been found.

    // Draw a thumbnail of the target in the upper-left
    // corner so that the user knows what it is.

    int height = mReferenceImage.height();
    int width = mReferenceImage.width();
    int maxDimension = Math.min(dst.width(),
      dst.height()) / 2;
    double aspectRatio = width / (double)height;
    if (height > width) {
      height = maxDimension;
      width = (int)(height * aspectRatio);
    } else {
      width = maxDimension;
      height = (int)(width / aspectRatio);
    }
    Mat dstROI = dst.submat(0, height, 0, width);
    Imgproc.resize(mReferenceImage, dstROI, dstROI.size(),
      0.0, 0.0, Imgproc.INTER_AREA);

    return;
  }

  // Outline the found target in green.
  Core.line(dst, new Point(mSceneCorners.get(0, 0)),
    new Point(mSceneCorners.get(1, 0)), mLineColor, 4);
  Core.line(dst, new Point(mSceneCorners.get(1, 0)),
    new Point(mSceneCorners.get(2, 0)), mLineColor, 4);
```

```
    Core.line(dst, new Point(mSceneCorners.get(2, 0)),
      new Point(mSceneCorners.get(3, 0)), mLineColor, 4);
    Core.line(dst, new Point(mSceneCorners.get(3,0)),
      new Point(mSceneCorners.get(0, 0)), mLineColor, 4);
  }
}
```

Although `ImageDetectionFilter` has a more complicated implementation than our previous filters, it still has a simple interface. Just instantiate it with a drawable resource, and then apply the filter to source and destination images as needed.

Adding the tracker filters to CameraActivity

To use instances of `ImageDetectionFilter`, we make the same kind of modifications to `CameraActivity` as we did for other filters in the previous chapter. Recall that all our filter classes implement the `Filter` interface so that `CameraActivity` can use them all in similar ways.

First, we need to define some text (for the menu button) in `res/values/strings.xml`:

```
<string name="menu_next_image_detection_filter">Next
  Tracker</string>
```

Next, we need to define the menu button itself in `res/menu/activity_camera.xml`:

```
<menu xmlns:android="http://schemas.android.com/apk/res/android">
  <item
    android:id="@+id/menu_next_image_detection_filter"
    android:orderInCategory="100"
    android:showAsAction="ifRoom|withText"
    android:title="@string/menu_next_image_detection_filter" />
  <!-- ... -->
</menu>
```

The rest of our modifications pertain to `CameraActivity.java`. We need to add new member variables to keep track of the selected image detection filter:

```
// Keys for storing the indices of the active filters.
private static final String STATE_IMAGE_DETECTION_FILTER_INDEX =
  "imageDetectionFilterIndex";
private static final String STATE_CURVE_FILTER_INDEX =
```

```
    "curveFilterIndex";
  private static final String STATE_MIXER_FILTER_INDEX =
    "mixerFilterIndex";
  private static final String STATE_CONVOLUTION_FILTER_INDEX =
    "convolutionFilterIndex";

  // The filters.
  private Filter[] mImageDetectionFilters;
  private Filter[] mCurveFilters;
  private Filter[] mMixerFilters;
  private Filter[] mConvolutionFilters;

  // The indices of the active filters.
  private int mImageDetectionFilterIndex;
  private int mCurveFilterIndex;
  private int mMixerFilterIndex;
  private int mConvolutionFilterIndex;
```

Once OpenCV is initialized, we need to instantiate all of the image detection filters and put them in an array. For brevity, I have added just two image detection filters as examples but you can easily modify the following code to support tracking of more images, or different images:

```
public void onManagerConnected(final int status) {
  switch (status) {
    case LoaderCallbackInterface.SUCCESS:
      Log.d(TAG, "OpenCV loaded successfully");
      mCameraView.enableView();
      mBgr = new Mat();

      final Filter starryNight;
       try {
         starryNight = new ImageDetectionFilter(
           CameraActivity.this,
             R.drawable.starry_night);
      } catch (IOException e) {
        Log.e(TAG, "Failed to load drawable: " +
          "starry_night");
        e.printStackTrace();
        break;
      }
```

```
         mImageDetectionFilters = new Filter[] {
           new NoneFilter(),
             starryNight,
               akbarHunting
         };

         // ...
      }
    }
  };
```

When the activity is created, we need to load any saved data about the selected image detection filter:

```
protected void onCreate(final Bundle savedInstanceState) {
  super.onCreate(savedInstanceState);

  final Window window = getWindow();
  window.addFlags(
    WindowManager.LayoutParams.FLAG_KEEP_SCREEN_ON);

  if (savedInstanceState != null) {
    mCameraIndex = savedInstanceState.getInt(
      STATE_CAMERA_INDEX, 0);
    mImageDetectionFilterIndex = savedInstanceState.getInt(
      STATE_IMAGE_DETECTION_FILTER_INDEX, 0);
    mCurveFilterIndex = savedInstanceState.getInt(
      STATE_CURVE_FILTER_INDEX, 0);
    mMixerFilterIndex = savedInstanceState.getInt(
      STATE_MIXER_FILTER_INDEX, 0);
    mConvolutionFilterIndex = savedInstanceState.getInt(
      STATE_CONVOLUTION_FILTER_INDEX, 0);
  } else {
    mCameraIndex = 0;
    mImageDetectionFilterIndex = 0;
    mCurveFilterIndex = 0;
    mMixerFilterIndex = 0;
    mConvolutionFilterIndex = 0;
  }

  // ...
}
```

Conversely, before the activity is destroyed, we need to save data about the selected image detection filter:

```
public void onSaveInstanceState(Bundle savedInstanceState) {
  // Save the current camera index.
  savedInstanceState.putInt(STATE_CAMERA_INDEX, mCameraIndex);

  // Save the current filter indices.
  savedInstanceState.putInt(STATE_IMAGE_DETECTION_FILTER_INDEX,
    mImageDetectionFilterIndex);
  savedInstanceState.putInt(STATE_CURVE_FILTER_INDEX,
    mCurveFilterIndex);
  savedInstanceState.putInt(STATE_MIXER_FILTER_INDEX,
    mMixerFilterIndex);
  savedInstanceState.putInt(STATE_CONVOLUTION_FILTER_INDEX,
    mConvolutionFilterIndex);

  super.onSaveInstanceState(savedInstanceState);
}
```

When the **Next Tracker** menu button is pressed, the selected image detection filter needs to be updated:

```
public boolean onOptionsItemSelected(final MenuItem item) {
  if (mIsMenuLocked) {
    return true;
  }
  switch (item.getItemId()) {
  case R.id.menu_next_image_detection_filter:
    mImageDetectionFilterIndex++;
    if (mImageDetectionFilterIndex ==
      mImageDetectionFilters.length) {
      mImageDetectionFilterIndex = 0;
    }
    return true;
  // ...
  default:
    return super.onOptionsItemSelected(item);
  }
}
```

Finally, when the camera captures a frame, the selected image detection filter needs to be applied to the frame. To ensure that other filters do not interfere with the image detection, it is important to apply the image detection filter first:

```java
public Mat onCameraFrame(final CvCameraViewFrame inputFrame) {
    final Mat rgba = inputFrame.rgba();

    // Apply the active filters.
    if (mImageDetectionFilters != null) {
        mImageDetectionFilters[mImageDetectionFilterIndex].apply(
            rgba, rgba);
    }
    if (mCurveFilters != null) {
        mCurveFilters[mCurveFilterIndex].apply(rgba, rgba);
    }
    if (mMixerFilters != null) {
        mMixerFilters[mMixerFilterIndex].apply(rgba, rgba);
    }
    if (mConvolutionFilters != null) {
        mConvolutionFilters[mConvolutionFilterIndex].apply(
            rgba, rgba);
    }

    if (mIsPhotoPending) {
        mIsPhotoPending = false;
        takePhoto(rgba);
    }

    if (mIsCameraFrontFacing) {
        // Mirror (horizontally flip) the preview.
        Core.flip(rgba, rgba, 1);
    }

    return rgba;
}
```

That's all! Print the target images or display them on-screen. Then, run the app, select an appropriate image detection filter, and point the camera at the target. Depending on your Android device, you might need to hold it still for a second or two in order for the camera to focus on the target. Then, you should see the target outlined in green. For example, see the outline around *The Starry Night* in the following screenshot:

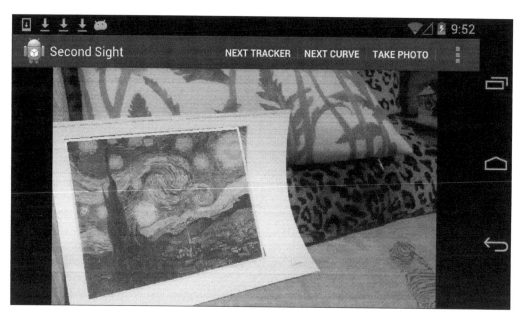

Summary

The Second Sight app can see now! At least, it can recognize any image from a predefined set and can draw a quadrilateral around that image. To a certain extent, this feature is robust with respect to scale, rotation, and skew. For example, the image can be tracked from various distances and angles of view.

Although we only added a single class in this chapter, we covered a lot of OpenCV functionality. Next, we will step back and consider how to integrate this OpenCV functionality with other types of interactive graphics. We will build a small game atop image recognition filters of Second Sight.

5

Combining Image Tracking with 3D Rendering

Our goal in this chapter is to combine image tracking with 3D rendering. We will modify our existing image tracker so that it fully determines the target's position and rotation in 3D. Then, using Android SDK's implementation of OpenGL ES, we will draw a 3D cube sitting atop the tracked image. This is a case of **augmented reality (AR)**, meaning that we are superimposing a virtual object (the cube) on a specific part of a real scene.

 The complete Eclipse project for this chapter can be downloaded from my website at http://nummist.com/opencv/5206_05.zip.

Adding files to the project

For this chapter, we will modify our existing `ImageDetectionFilter` class. We will also add files for the following new classes and interfaces:

- `com.nummist.secondsight.ARCubeRenderer`: A class representing the rendering logic for a cube that sits atop a tracked, real-world object. The class implements the `GLSurfaceView.Renderer` interface from the Android standard library. The projection matrix is determined by a `CameraProjectionAdapter` instance, and the cube's pose matrix is determined by an `ARFilter` instance, as described later.

- `com.nummist.secondsight.adapters.CameraProjectionAdapter`: A class representing the relationship between a physical camera and a projection matrix. The projection matrix may be fetched in either OpenCV or OpenGL format.

- `com.nummist.secondsight.filters.ar.ARFilter`: An interface representing a filter that captures the position and rotation of a real-world object as an OpenGL matrix. We will modify `ImageDetectionFilter` to implement this interface.

- `com.nummist.secondsight.filters.ar.NoneARFilter`: A class representing a filter that does nothing. It extends the `NoneFilter` class and implements the `ARFilter` interface. We use `NoneARFilter` when we want to turn off filtering but still have an object that conforms to the `ARFilter` interface.

Together, these types support the rendering of a virtual 3D environment that is consistent with certain properties of the real video camera and scene.

Defining the ARFilter interface

Given a source image, our previous filters just produced a destination image. Now, we also want to produce data about the pose (position and rotation) of something that may be visible in the source image. For OpenGL's purposes, a pose is expressed as an array of 16 floating point numbers, representing a 4 x 4 transformation matrix. Thus, we may define the `ARFilter` interface as follows:

 If you are unfamiliar with vector algebra and matrix algebra, as they apply to 3D geometry, you might find parts of this chapter hard to follow. Roughly speaking, you can imagine a transformation matrix as a table containing values that are based on the three coordinates of a 3D position and on trigonometric functions of the three angles of a 3D rotation. Two transformations can be applied consecutively by matrix multiplication. For a primer on these topics, see the online tutorial *Vector Math for 3D Computer Graphics* at http://chortle.ccsu.edu/vectorlessons/vectorindex.html.

```
public interface ARFilter extends Filter {
    public float[] getGLPose();
}
```

When the pose matrix is unknown, `getGLPose()` should return `null`.

The most basic implementation of the `ARFilter` interface is the `NoneARFilter` class. `NoneARFilter` does not actually find the pose matrix. Instead, the `getGLPose()` method always returns `null`, as we can see in the following code:

```
public class NoneARFilter extends NoneFilter implements ARFilter {
  @Override
  public float[] getGLPose() {
    return null;
  }
}
```

The `NoneARFilter` class, similar to its parent class `NoneFilter`, is just a convenient stand-in for other filters. We use `NoneARFilter` when we want to turn off filtering but still have an object that conforms to the `ARFilter` interface.

Building projection matrices in CameraProjectionAdapter

Here is an exercise for sightseers. Choose a famous photo that was taken at a recognizable location, somewhere that should still look similar today. Travel to that site and explore it until you know how the photographer set up the shot. Where was the camera positioned and how was it rotated?

If you found an answer, and if you are sure of it, you must have already known which lens or zoom setting the photographer used. Without that information, you could not have narrowed down the feasible camera poses to the one, true pose.

We face a similar problem when trying to determine the pose of a photographed object relative to a monocular (single-lens) camera. To find a unique solution, we first need to know the camera's horizontal and vertical field of view, and horizontal and vertical resolution in pixels.

Fortunately, we can get these data via the `android.hardware.Camera.Parameters` class. Our `CameraProjectionAdapter` class will allow client code to provide a `Camera.Parameters` object and then get a projection matrix in either OpenCV or OpenGL format.

Unfortunately, on some devices, the data provided by `Camera.Parameters` are misleading or just plain wrong.

On a device with a zoom lens, the horizontal and vertical fields of view may be based on the lens's widest (1x) zoom setting. For advice on finding fields of view based on the current zoom setting, see the following StackOverflow thread at `http://stackoverflow.com/questions/3261776/determine-angle-of-view-of-smartphone-camera`.

On some devices, the fields of view are reported as 360 degrees or other invalid/incorrect values. For example, the Sony Xperia Arc may report 360 degree fields of view.

As an alternative to relying on `Camera.Parameters`, we could require the user to calibrate the camera at runtime. OpenCV provides calibration functions that require the user to take a picture of a chessboard. We do not cover these functions in this book but you can read about them in the official documentation at `http://docs.opencv.org/doc/tutorials/calib3d/camera_calibration/camera_calibration.html` or in other OpenCV books such as *OpenCV 2 Computer Vision Application Programming Cookbook* (Packt Publishing), by Robert Laganière.

As member variables, `CameraProjection` stores all the data that it needs to construct the projection matrices. It also stores the matrices themselves, and Boolean flags to indicate whether the matrices are dirty (whether they need to be reconstructed the next time that client code fetches them). Let's write the following declaration of the class and member variables:

```
public class CameraProjectionAdapter {

    float mFOVY = 43.6f; // 30mm equivalent
    float mFOVX = 65.4f; // 30mm equivalent
    int mHeightPx = 640;
    int mWidthPx = 480;
    float mNear = 1f;
    float mFar = 10000f;

    final float[] mProjectionGL = new float[16];
    boolean mProjectionDirtyGL = true;

    MatOfDouble mProjectionCV;
    boolean mProjectionDirtyCV = true;
```

Note that we assume some default values, just in case the client code fails to provide a `Camera.Parameters` instance. Also note that the `mNear` and `mFar` variables store the near and far **clipping distances**, meaning that the OpenGL camera will not render anything nearer or farther than these respective distances. We can declare the class and member variables as follows:

```
public void setCameraParameters(Parameters parameters) {
    mFOVY = parameters.getVerticalViewAngle();
    mFOVX = parameters.getHorizontalViewAngle();

    Size pictureSize = parameters.getPictureSize();
    mHeightPx = pictureSize.height;
    mWidthPx = pictureSize.width;

    mProjectionDirtyGL = true;
    mProjectionDirtyCV = true;
}
```

For the near and far clipping distances, we just need a simple setter, which we can implement as follows:

```
public void setClipDistances(float near, float far) {
    mNear = near;
    mFar = far;
    mProjectionDirtyGL = true;
}
```

Since the clipping distances are only relevant to OpenGL, we set the dirty flag for only the OpenGL matrix.

Next, let's consider the getter for the OpenGL projection matrix. If the matrix is dirty, we reconstruct it. For constructing a projection matrix, OpenGL provides a function called `frustumM(float[] m, int offset, float left, float right, float bottom, float top, float near, float far)`. The first two arguments are an array and offset where the matrix data should be stored. The rest of the arguments describe the edges of the **view frustum**, which is the region of space that the camera can see. Although you might be tempted to think that this region is conical, it is actually a truncated pyramid, due to near and far clipping, and the rectangular shape of the user's screen. Here is a visualization of the view frustum:

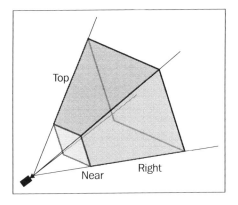

Based on the clipping distances and the fields of view, we can find the view frustum's other measurements by simple trigonometry, as seen in the following implementation:

```
public float[] getProjectionGL() {
    if (mProjectionDirtyGL) {
        final float top =
            (float)Math.tan(mFOVY * Math.PI / 360f) * mNear;
        final float right =
            (float)Math.tan(mFOVX * Math.PI / 360f) * mNear;
        Matrix.frustumM(mProjectionGL, 0,
            -right, right, -top, top, mNear, mFar);
        mProjectionDirtyGL = false;
    }
    return mProjectionGL;
}
```

The getter for the OpenCV projection matrix is slightly more complicated because the library does not offer a similar helper function for constructing the matrix. Thus, we must understand the contents of the OpenCV projection matrix and construct it ourselves. It has the following 3 x 3 format:

```
focalLengthXInPixels    0                       centerXInPixels
0                       focalLengthYInPixels    centerYInPixels
0                       0                       1
```

For a symmetrical lens system (which ought to be the norm), the matrix format simplifies to the following:

```
focalLengthInPixels    0                      (0.5 * widthInPixels)
0                      focalLengthInPixels    (0.5 * heightInPixels)
0                      0                      1
```

Focal length is the distance between the camera's sensor and the rear lens element. For OpenCV's purposes, the focal length is expressed in **pixel-related units**. Notionally, we could attribute a physical size to a pixel, by dividing the camera sensor's width or height by its horizontal or vertical resolution. However, since we do not know any physical measurements of the sensor or lens system, we instead use trigonometry to determine the pixel-related focal length. The implementation is as follows:

```
public MatOfDouble getProjectionCV() {
    if (mProjectionDirtyCV) {
        if (mProjectionCV == null) {
            mProjectionCV = new MatOfDouble();
            mProjectionCV.create(3, 3, CvType.CV_64FC1);
        }
```

```
        double diagonalPx = Math.sqrt(
          (Math.pow(mWidthPx, 2.0) +
            Math.pow(mHeightPx, 2.0)));
        double diagonalFOV = Math.sqrt(
          (Math.pow(mFOVX, 2.0) +
            Math.pow(mFOVY, 2.0)));
        double focalLengthPx = diagonalPx /
          (2.0 * Math.tan(0.5 * diagonalFOV));

        mProjectionCV.put(0, 0, focalLengthPx);
        mProjectionCV.put(0, 1, 0.0);
        mProjectionCV.put(0, 2, 0.5 * mWidthPx);
        mProjectionCV.put(1, 0, 0.0);
        mProjectionCV.put(1, 1, focalLengthPx);
        mProjectionCV.put(1, 2, 0.5 * mHeightPx);
        mProjectionCV.put(2, 0, 0.0);
        mProjectionCV.put(2, 1, 0.0);
        mProjectionCV.put(2, 2, 0.0);
    }
    return mProjectionCV;
  }
}
```

Client code can use `CameraProjectionAdapter` by instantiating it, calling `setCameraParameters` whenever the active camera changes, and calling `getProjectionGL` and `getProjectionCV` whenever a projection matrix is needed for OpenGL or OpenCV computations.

Modifying ImageDetectionFilter for 3D tracking

For 3D tracking, `ImageDetectionFilter` needs all the same member variables as before, plus several more to store computations about the target's pose. Moreover, the class needs to implement the `ARFilter` interface. Let's modify `ImageDetectionFilter` as follows:

```
public class ImageDetectionFilter implements ARFilter {

  // ...

  private final MatOfDouble mDistCoeffs = new MatOfDouble(
    0.0, 0.0, 0.0, 0.0);
```

```
private final CameraProjectionAdapter mCameraProjectionAdapter;
private final MatOfDouble mRVec = new MatOfDouble();
private final MatOfDouble mTVec = new MatOfDouble();
private final MatOfDouble mRotation = new MatOfDouble();
private final float[] mGLPose = new float[16];

private boolean mTargetFound = false;
```

The constructor should require an instance of `CameraProjectionAdapter` as an additional argument. We store it in a member variable, as seen in the following code:

```
public ImageDetectionFilter(final Context context,
    final int referenceImageResourceID,
        final CameraProjectionAdapter cameraProjectionAdapter)
            throws IOException {

    // ...

    mCameraProjectionAdapter = cameraProjectionAdapter;
}
```

To satisfy the `ARFilter` interface, we need to implement a getter for the OpenGL pose matrix. When the target is lost, this getter should return `null` because we have no valid data about the pose. We can implement the getter as follows:

```
@Override
public float[] getGLPose() {
    return (mTargetFound ? mGLPose : null);
}
```

Let's rename our `findHomography` method to `findPose`. To reflect this name change, the implementation of the `apply` method changes as follows:

```
@Override
public void apply(final Mat src, final Mat dst) {
    Imgproc.cvtColor(src, mGraySrc, Imgproc.COLOR_RGBA2GRAY);

    mFeatureDetector.detect(mGraySrc, mSceneKeypoints);
    mDescriptorExtractor.compute(mGraySrc, mSceneKeypoints,
        mSceneDescriptors);
    mDescriptorMatcher.match(mSceneDescriptors,
        mReferenceDescriptors, mMatches);

    findPose();
    draw(src, dst);
}
```

After finding keypoints, the implementation of `findPose` starts to differ from the old `findHomography` method. We convert the reference keypoints to 3D (with a z value of 0), for using in 3D computations. Then, we get an OpenCV projection matrix from our instance of `CameraProjectionAdapter`. Next, we solve for the target's position and rotation, based on the matching keypoints and the projection. Most of the calculations are done by an OpenCV function called `Calib3d.solvePnP(MatOfPoint3f objectPoints, MatOfPoint2f imagePoints, Mat cameraMatrix, MatOfDouble distCoeffs, Mat rvec, Mat tvec)`. This function puts the position and rotation results in two separate vectors. The y and z directions in OpenCV are inverted compared to OpenGL, so we need to multiply these components of the vectors by -1. We convert the rotation vector into a matrix using another OpenCV function called `Calib3d.Rodrigues(Mat src, Mat dst)`. Last, we manually convert the resulting rotation matrix and position vector into a `float[16]` array that is appropriate for OpenGL. The code is as follows:

```java
private void findPose() {

    // ...

    // Identify "good" keypoints based on match distance.
    List<Point3> goodReferencePointsList =
        new ArrayList<Point3>();
    ArrayList<Point> goodScenePointsList =
        new ArrayList<Point>();
    double maxGoodMatchDist = 1.75 * minDist;
    for(DMatch match : matchesList) {
        if (match.distance < maxGoodMatchDist) {
            Point point =
                referenceKeypointsList.get(match.trainIdx).pt;
            Point3 point3 = new Point3(point.x, point.y, 0.0);
            goodReferencePointsList.add(point3);
            goodScenePointsList.add(
                sceneKeypointsList.get(match.queryIdx).pt);
        }
    }

    if (goodReferencePointsList.size() < 4 ||
        goodScenePointsList.size() < 4) {
        // There are too few good points to find the pose.
        return;
    }
```

```java
MatOfPoint3f goodReferencePoints = new MatOfPoint3f();
goodReferencePoints.fromList(goodReferencePointsList);

MatOfPoint2f goodScenePoints = new MatOfPoint2f();
goodScenePoints.fromList(goodScenePointsList);

MatOfDouble projection =
  mCameraProjectionAdapter.getProjectionCV();
Calib3d.solvePnP(goodReferencePoints, goodScenePoints,
  projection, mDistCoeffs, mRVec, mTVec);

double[] rVecArray = mRVec.toArray();
rVecArray[1] *= -1.0;
rVecArray[2] *= -1.0;
mRVec.fromArray(rVecArray);

Calib3d.Rodrigues(mRVec, mRotation);

double[] tVecArray = mTVec.toArray();

mGLPose[0]  =  (float)mRotation.get(0, 0)[0];
mGLPose[1]  =  (float)mRotation.get(1, 0)[0];
mGLPose[2]  =  (float)mRotation.get(2, 0)[0];
mGLPose[3]  =  0f;
mGLPose[4]  =  (float)mRotation.get(0, 1)[0];
mGLPose[5]  =  (float)mRotation.get(1, 1)[0];
mGLPose[6]  =  (float)mRotation.get(2, 1)[0];
mGLPose[7]  =  0f;
mGLPose[8]  =  (float)mRotation.get(0, 2)[0];
mGLPose[9]  =  (float)mRotation.get(1, 2)[0];
mGLPose[10] =  (float)mRotation.get(2, 2)[0];
mGLPose[11] =  0f;
mGLPose[12] =  (float)tVecArray[0];
mGLPose[13] = -(float)tVecArray[1];
mGLPose[14] = -(float)tVecArray[2];
mGLPose[15] =  1f;

mTargetFound = true;
}
```

Last, let's modify our `draw` method by removing the code that draws a green border around the tracked image. (Instead, the `ARCubeRenderer` class will be responsible for drawing a cube atop the tracked image.) After removing the unwanted code, we are left with the following implementation of the `draw` method:

```
protected void draw(Mat src, Mat dst) {

    if (dst != src) {
        src.copyTo(dst);
    }

    if (!mTargetFound) {
        // The target has not been found.

        // Draw a thumbnail of the target in the upper-left
        // corner so that the user knows what it is.

        int height = mReferenceImage.height();
        int width = mReferenceImage.width();
        int maxDimension = Math.min(dst.width(),
            dst.height()) / 2;
        double aspectRatio = width / (double)height;
        if (height > width) {
            height = maxDimension;
            width = (int)(height * aspectRatio);
        } else {
            width = maxDimension;
            height = (int)(width / aspectRatio);
        }
        Mat dstROI = dst.submat(0, height, 0, width);
        Imgproc.resize(mReferenceImage, dstROI, dstROI.size(),
            0.0, 0.0, Imgproc.INTER_AREA);
    }
  }
}
```

Next, we look at how to render the cube with OpenGL.

Rendering the cube in ARCubeRenderer

Android provides a class called `GLSurfaceView`, which is a widget that is drawn by OpenGL. The drawing logic is encapsulated via an interface called `GLSurfaceView.Renderer`, which we will implement in `ARCubeRenderer`. The interface requires the following methods:

- `onDrawFrame(GL10 gl)`: It is called to draw the current frame.

- `onSurfaceChanged(GL10 gl, int width, int height)`: It is called when the surface size changes. For our purposes, this method does not need to do anything.

- `onSurfaceCreated(GL10 gl, EGLConfig config)`: It is called when the surface is created or recreated. For our purposes, this method does not need to do anything.

The `GL10` instance, which is passed as an argument, provides access to the standard OpenGL ES 1.0 functionality. Basically, we are interested in two kinds of OpenGL functionality; applying matrix transformations to 3D vertices and then drawing triangles based on the transformed vertices. Our cube will have eight vertices and 12 triangles (six square faces * two triangles per square face). We will specify a color for each vertex and we will describe the triangles in a format called a **triangle fan**. A triangle fan is an array of 3 or more vertices. For each vertex `v[i]` in the fan, where `i >= 2`, a triangle is formed by `v[0]`, `v[i-1]`, and `v[i]`.

Taking any vertex in the cube, we may imagine six triangles (three square faces) fanning out from that vertex. Thus, two triangle fans are enough to specify the 12 triangles, provided that we start the fans from opposite corners of the cube.

Vertices, vertex colors, and triangle fans are all stored in `ByteBuffer` instances. Since we only support one style of cube, we will use static instances of `ByteBuffer` so that multiple `ARCubeRenderer` instances may share them. As member variables, we also want `ARFilter` to provide the cube's pose matrix, a `CameraProjectionAdapter` to provide the projection matrix, and a scale to allow client code to resize the cube. The declarations of `ARCubeRenderer` and its variables are as follows:

```java
public class ARCubeRenderer implements GLSurfaceView.Renderer {

    public ARFilter filter;
    public CameraProjectionAdapter cameraProjectionAdapter;
    public float scale = 100f;

    private static final ByteBuffer VERTICES;
    private static final ByteBuffer COLORS;
    private static final ByteBuffer TRIANGLE_FAN_0;
    private static final ByteBuffer TRIANGLE_FAN_1;
```

Since the vertices, colors, and triangle fans are `static` variables, we initialize them in a `static` block. For each buffer, we must specify the required number of bytes. The vertices take up 96 bytes (8 vertices * 3 floats per vertex * 4 bytes per float). We specify vertices for a cube that is 2 units wide. After populating the buffer, we rewind its pointer to the first index. The code is as follows:

```
static {
  VERTICES = ByteBuffer.allocateDirect(96);
  VERTICES.order(ByteOrder.nativeOrder());
  VERTICES.asFloatBuffer().put(new float[] {
    -1f,  1f,  1f,
     1f,  1f,  1f,
     1f, -1f,  1f,
    -1f, -1f,  1f,

    -1f,  1f, -1f,
     1f,  1f, -1f,
     1f, -1f, -1f,
    -1f, -1f, -1f
  });
  VERTICES.position(0);
```

The vertex colors take up 32 bytes (8 vertices * 4 bytes of RGBA color per vertex). We specify a different color for each vertex, as seen in the following code:

```
COLORS = ByteBuffer.allocateDirect(32);
COLORS.put(new byte[] {
  // yellow
  Byte.MAX_VALUE, Byte.MAX_VALUE, 0, Byte.MAX_VALUE,
  // cyan
  0, Byte.MAX_VALUE, Byte.MAX_VALUE, Byte.MAX_VALUE,
  // black
  0, 0, 0, Byte.MAX_VALUE,
  // magenta
  Byte.MAX_VALUE, 0, Byte.MAX_VALUE, Byte.MAX_VALUE,

  Byte.MAX_VALUE, 0, 0, Byte.MAX_VALUE, // red
  0, Byte.MAX_VALUE, 0, Byte.MAX_VALUE, // green
  0, 0, Byte.MAX_VALUE, Byte.MAX_VALUE, // blue
  0, 0, 0, Byte.MAX_VALUE // black
});
COLORS.position(0);
```

The two triangle fans take up 18 bytes each (6 triangles * 3 vertex indices per triangle). We specify fans that are based at the cube's far upper-right and near lower-left corners, as seen in the following code:

```
TRIANGLE_FAN_0 = ByteBuffer.allocate(18);
TRIANGLE_FAN_0.put(new byte[] {
    1, 0, 3,
    1, 3, 2,
    1, 2, 6,
    1, 6, 5,
    1, 5, 4,
    1, 4, 0
});
TRIANGLE_FAN_0.position(0);

TRIANGLE_FAN_1 = ByteBuffer.allocate(18);
TRIANGLE_FAN_1.put(new byte[] {
    7, 4, 5,
    7, 5, 6,
    7, 6, 2,
    7, 2, 3,
    7, 3, 0,
    7, 0, 4
});
TRIANGLE_FAN_1.position(0);
}
```

When drawing to an instance of `GLSurfaceView`, we first clear any previous content by replacing it with a fully transparent color. Then, we check whether a projection matrix and pose matrix are available. If they are, we tell OpenGL to use these matrices and to also move and scale the cube so that we have an appropriately sized cube sitting atop the target. Then, we supply the vertices and vertex colors to OpenGL and tell it to draw the triangle fans. The implementation is as follows:

```
@Override
public void onDrawFrame(final GL10 gl) {

    gl.glClear(GL10.GL_COLOR_BUFFER_BIT |
        GL10.GL_DEPTH_BUFFER_BIT);
    gl.glClearColor(0f, 0f, 0f, 0f); // transparent

    if (filter == null) {
        return;
    }
```

```
    if (cameraProjectionAdapter == null) {
      return;
    }

    float[] pose = filter.getGLPose();
    if (pose == null) {
      return;
    }

    gl.glMatrixMode(GL10.GL_PROJECTION);
    float[] projection =
      cameraProjectionAdapter.getProjectionGL();
    gl.glLoadMatrixf(projection, 0);

    gl.glMatrixMode(GL10.GL_MODELVIEW);
    gl.glLoadMatrixf(pose, 0);
    gl.glTranslatef(0f, 0f, 1f);
    gl.glScalef(scale, scale, scale);

    gl.glEnableClientState(GL10.GL_VERTEX_ARRAY);
    gl.glEnableClientState(GL10.GL_COLOR_ARRAY);

    gl.glVertexPointer(3, GL11.GL_FLOAT, 0, VERTICES);
    gl.glColorPointer(4, GL11.GL_UNSIGNED_BYTE, 0, COLORS);

    gl.glDrawElements(GL10.GL_TRIANGLE_FAN, 18,
      GL10.GL_UNSIGNED_BYTE, TRIANGLE_FAN_0);
    gl.glDrawElements(GL10.GL_TRIANGLE_FAN, 18,
      GL10.GL_UNSIGNED_BYTE, TRIANGLE_FAN_1);
  }
```

Finally, to satisfy the rest of the `GLSurfaceView.Renderer` interface, we provide empty implementations of `onSurfaceChanged` and `onSurfaceCreated`, as seen in the following code:

```
  @Override
  public void onSurfaceChanged(final GL10 gl, final int width,
    final int height) {
  }

  @Override
  public void onSurfaceCreated(final GL10 arg0,
    final EGLConfig config) {

  }
```

Now, we are ready to integrate 3D tracking and rendering into our application.

Adding 3D tracking and rendering to CameraActivity

We need to make a few changes to `CameraActivity` to conform with our changes to `ImageDetectionFilter` and with the new interface provided by `ARFilter`. We also need to modify the activity's layout so that it includes a `GLSurfaceView`. The adapter for this `GLSurfaceView` will be `ARCubeRenderer`. The `ImageDetectionFilter` and the `ARCubeRenderer` methods will use `CameraProjectionAdapter` to coordinate their projection matrices.

First, let's make the following changes to the member variables of `CameraActivity`:

```
// The filters.
private ARFilter[] mImageDetectionFilters;
private Filter[] mCurveFilters;
private Filter[] mMixerFilters;
private Filter[] mConvolutionFilters;

// ...

// The camera view.
private CameraBridgeViewBase mCameraView;

// An adapter between the video camera and projection matrix.
private CameraProjectionAdapter mCameraProjectionAdapter;

// The renderer for 3D augmentations.
private ARCubeRenderer mARRenderer;
```

As usual, once the OpenCV library is loaded, we need to create the filters. The only changes are that we need to pass an instance of `CameraProjectionAdapter` to each constructor of `ImageDetectionFilter`, and we need to use a `NoneARFilter` in place of a `NoneFilter`. The code is as follows:

```
public void onManagerConnected(final int status) {
  switch (status) {
    case LoaderCallbackInterface.SUCCESS:
    Log.d(TAG, "OpenCV loaded successfully");
    mCameraView.enableView();
    mBgr = new Mat();

    final ARFilter starryNight;
    try {
      starryNight = new ImageDetectionFilter(
```

```
            CameraActivity.this,
              R.drawable.starry_night,
                mCameraProjectionAdapter);
        } catch (IOException e) {
          Log.e(TAG, "Failed to load drawable: " +
            "starry_night");
          e.printStackTrace();
          break;
        }

        final ARFilter akbarHunting;
        try {
          akbarHunting = new ImageDetectionFilter(
            CameraActivity.this,
              R.drawable.akbar_hunting_with_cheetahs,
                mCameraProjectionAdapter);
        } catch (IOException e) {
          Log.e(TAG, "Failed to load drawable: " +
            "akbar_hunting_with_cheetahs");
          e.printStackTrace();
          break;
        }

        mImageDetectionFilters = new ARFilter[] {
          new NoneARFilter(),
          starryNight,
          akbarHunting
        };

    // ...
    }
  }
```

The remaining changes belong in the `onCreate` method, where we should create and configure the instances of `GLSurfaceView`, `ARCubeRenderer`, and `CameraProjectionAdapter`. The implementation includes some boilerplate code to overlay an instance of `GLSurfaceView` atop an instance of `NativeCameraView`. These two views are contained inside a standard Android layout widget called a `FrameLayout`. After setting up the layout, we need a `Camera` instance and a `Camera.Parameters` instance in order to do our remaining configuration. The `Camera` instance is obtained via a static method, `Camera.open()`, which may take a camera index as an optional argument on Android 2.3 and later. (By default, the first rear-facing camera is used.) When we are done with the `Camera`, we must call its `release()` method in order to make it available later. The code is as follows:

Every call to `Camera.open` must be paired with a call to the `Camera` instance's `release` method. Otherwise, our app and other apps may subsequently encounter a `RuntimeException` while calling `Camera.open`. For more details about the `Camera` class, see the official documentation at `http://developer.android.com/reference/android/hardware/Camera.html`.

```java
protected void onCreate(final Bundle savedInstanceState) {
    super.onCreate(savedInstanceState);

    // ...

    FrameLayout layout = new FrameLayout(this);
    layout.setLayoutParams(new FrameLayout.LayoutParams(
        FrameLayout.LayoutParams.MATCH_PARENT,
            FrameLayout.LayoutParams.MATCH_PARENT));
    setContentView(layout);

    mCameraView = new NativeCameraView(this, mCameraIndex);
    mCameraView.setCvCameraViewListener(this);
    mCameraView.setLayoutParams(new FrameLayout.LayoutParams(
        FrameLayout.LayoutParams.MATCH_PARENT,
            FrameLayout.LayoutParams.MATCH_PARENT));
    layout.addView(mCameraView);

    GLSurfaceView glSurfaceView = new GLSurfaceView(this);
    glSurfaceView.getHolder().setFormat(
        PixelFormat.TRANSPARENT);
    glSurfaceView.setEGLConfigChooser(8, 8, 8, 8, 0, 0);
    glSurfaceView.setZOrderOnTop(true);
    glSurfaceView.setLayoutParams(new FrameLayout.LayoutParams(
        FrameLayout.LayoutParams.MATCH_PARENT,
            FrameLayout.LayoutParams.MATCH_PARENT));
    layout.addView(glSurfaceView);

    mCameraProjectionAdapter = new CameraProjectionAdapter();

    mARRenderer = new ARCubeRenderer();
    mARRenderer.cameraProjectionAdapter =
        mCameraProjectionAdapter;
    glSurfaceView.setRenderer(mARRenderer);
```

```
final Camera camera;
if (Build.VERSION.SDK_INT >=
  Build.VERSION_CODES.GINGERBREAD) {
  CameraInfo cameraInfo = new CameraInfo();
  Camera.getCameraInfo(mCameraIndex, cameraInfo);
  mIsCameraFrontFacing =
    (cameraInfo.facing ==
      CameraInfo.CAMERA_FACING_FRONT);
  mNumCameras = Camera.getNumberOfCameras();
  camera = Camera.open(mCameraIndex);
} else { // pre-Gingerbread
  // Assume there is only 1 camera and it is rear-facing.
  mIsCameraFrontFacing = false;
  mNumCameras = 1;
  camera = Camera.open();
}
final Parameters parameters = camera.getParameters();
mCameraProjectionAdapter.setCameraParameters(
  parameters);
camera.release();
}
```

That's all! Run and test `Second Sight`. When you activate on of the instance of `ImageDetectionFilter` and hold the appropriate printed image in front of the camera, you should see a colorful cube rendered on top of the image. For example, see the following screenshot:

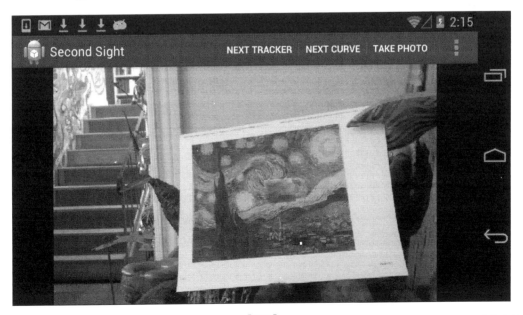

Learning more about 3D graphics on Android

Of course, in the world of 3D graphics, drawing a cube is similar to printing "Hello World"; it is just a basic demo. Although we have introduced meshes, transformations, and perspective, there are many other topics that we have not touched at all, such as lighting, materials (realistic-looking surfaces), and importing an artist's work from 3D art packages. For a deeper understanding of 3D graphics on Android, have a look at these books:

- *Pro OpenGL ES for Android* (Apress), by Mike Smithwick and Mayank Verma. This book covers Android's Java API for OpenGL ES.

- *OpenGL ES 2.0 Programming Guide* (Addison-Wesley), by Aaftab Munshi, Dan Ginsburg, and Dave Shreiner. This book covers the cross-platform C++ API for OpenGL ES.

- *Augmented Reality for Android Application Development* (Packt Publishing), by Jens Grubert and Dr. Raphael Grasset. This book shows how to use **JmonkeyEngine**, a cross-platform Java game engine, to render 3D graphics atop real-world images.

There are also many books on Android game development that may include a good introduction to 3D graphics.

Summary

We are now at the end of our introduction to OpenCV on Android. We have covered several major uses of OpenCV, including capturing camera input, applying effects to images, tracking images in 2D and 3D, and integrating with OpenGL for augmented reality rendering.

Taking the knowledge you have gained so far, you can go on to develop other OpenCV applications in Java, whether targeted at Android or other platforms. You might also wish to explore OpenCV's C++ version, which is likewise cross-platform and can interface with Android NDK.

Index

Thank you for buying
**Android Application
Programming with OpenCV**

About Packt Publishing

Packt, pronounced 'packed', published its first book "*Mastering phpMyAdmin for Effective MySQL Management*" in April 2004 and subsequently continued to specialize in publishing highly focused books on specific technologies and solutions.

Our books and publications share the experiences of your fellow IT professionals in adapting and customizing today's systems, applications, and frameworks. Our solution based books give you the knowledge and power to customize the software and technologies you're using to get the job done. Packt books are more specific and less general than the IT books you have seen in the past. Our unique business model allows us to bring you more focused information, giving you more of what you need to know, and less of what you don't.

Packt is a modern, yet unique publishing company, which focuses on producing quality, cutting-edge books for communities of developers, administrators, and newbies alike. For more information, please visit our website: www.packtpub.com.

Writing for Packt

We welcome all inquiries from people who are interested in authoring. Book proposals should be sent to author@packtpub.com. If your book idea is still at an early stage and you would like to discuss it first before writing a formal book proposal, contact us; one of our commissioning editors will get in touch with you.

We're not just looking for published authors; if you have strong technical skills but no writing experience, our experienced editors can help you develop a writing career, or simply get some additional reward for your expertise.

OpenCV Computer Vision with Python

ISBN: 978-1-782163-92-3   Paperback: 122 pages

Learn to capture videos, manipulate images, and track objects with Python using the OpenCV Library

1. Set up OpenCV, its Python bindings, and optional Kinect drivers on Windows, Mac or Ubuntu

2. Create an application that tracks and manipulates faces

3. Identify face regions using normal color images and depth images

Instant OpenCV Starter

ISBN: 978-1-782168-81-2   Paperback: 56 pages

Get started with OpenCV using practical, hands-on projects

1. Learn something new in an Instant! A short, fast, focused guide delivering immediate results

2. Step by step installation of OpenCV in Windows and Linux

3. Examples and code based on real-life implementation of OpenCV to help the reader understand the importance of this technology

4. Codes and algorithms with detailed explanations

Please check **www.PacktPub.com** for information on our titles

Mastering OpenCV with Practical Computer Vision Projects

ISBN: 978-1-849517-82-9   Paperback: 340 pages

Step-by-step tutorials to solve common real-world computer vision problems for desktop or mobile, from augmented reality and number plate recognition to face recognition and 3D head tracking

1. Allows anyone with basic OpenCV experience to rapidly obtain skills in many computer vision topics, for research or commercial use

2. Each chapter is a separate project covering a computer vision problem, written by a professional with proven experience on that topic

Android 4: New Features for Application Development

ISBN: 978-1-849519-52-6   Paperback: 166 pages

Develop Android applications using the new features of Android Ice Cream Sandwich

1. Learn new APIs in Android 4

2. Get familiar with the best practices in developing Android applications

3. Step-by-step approach with clearly explained sample codes

Please check **www.PacktPub.com** for information on our titles

36041084R00075